Learning from Academic Conferences

Critical Issues in the Future of Learning and Teaching

Editors

Britt-Marie Apelgren (*University of Gothenburg, Sweden*)
Pamela Burnard (*University of Cambridge, UK*)
Nese Cabaroglu (*University of Cukurova, Turkey*)
Pamela M. Denicolo (*University of Reading, UK*)
Nicola Simmons (*Brock University, Canada*)

Founding Editor

Michael Kompf† (*Brock University, Canada*)

VOLUME 16

The titles published in this series are listed at *brill.com/cifl*

Learning from Academic Conferences

Edited by

Celia Popovic

BRILL

SENSE

LEIDEN | BOSTON

Cover illustration: Drawing by Millie Popovic

All chapters in this book have undergone peer review.

The Library of Congress Cataloging-in-Publication Data is available online at http://catalog.loc.gov

Typeface for the Latin, Greek, and Cyrillic scripts: "Brill". See and download: brill.com/brill-typeface.

ISSN 2542-8721
ISBN 978-90-04-37299-3 (paperback)
ISBN 978-90-04-37300-6 (hardback)
ISBN 978-90-04-37301-3 (e-book)

To my parents,
Joy and Theo Hawkins

∴

Contents

Notes on Contributors

Sue Beckingham

For over a decade Sue has led Faculty Learning and Teaching Conferences and contributed to University wide events e.g. the international 'Social Media for Learning in Higher Education Conference'. She is a passionate advocate of social media pre/during/post conference to build community and conversations, and also to openly share valuable resources.

Fiona Campbell

Fiona says: I love conferences! Over many years I created, designed, contributed to and participated in a range of institutional, national and international conferences. As Co-Chair of the UK Staff and Educational Development Association Conference Committee, I had the good fortune to work with Celia to plan and deliver sectoral conferences. We also jointly conducted a funded international research project focused on the conference participant experience and the findings of that work have informed this book.

Alice L. E. V. Cassidy

Principal, In View Educational Development. Alice has been a presenter, keynote, field excursion leader and organizer at over 20 conferences since 1983. Serving as Vice-chair, Professional Development, EDC, 2006–2010, she created a conference handbook. She values working with students as co-scholars, networking and modeling sustainability by bringing her own dishes.

Beverley Hamilton

Academic Initiatives Officer in the Office of the Provost at the University of Windsor. Bev has contributed to the development, conceptualization, organization, and facilitation of national and international conferences and forums focused on the individual and systemic enhancement of teaching and learning.

Erika Kustra

Director, Teaching and Learning Development, Centre for Teaching and Learning, University of Windsor. Erika is the Chair of the Canadian Educational Developers Caucus. Over 20 years in educational development, Erika has helped organize national and international conferences with her colleagues, exploring approaches to enhance impact for participants and for larger culture change.

Celia Popovic

Director of the Teaching Commons at York University, Celia has had many years' experience organizing and attending conferences. She served as the co-chair conferences for SEDA (Staff and Educational Development Association) for 3 years and most recently was elected for a second term as Vice Chair Conferences for EDC (Educational Developers' Caucus).

Jessica Raffoul

is an Educational Consultant with the Centre for Teaching and Learning at the University of Windsor, Canada. Here, she contributes to and enhances research, programmes, and curricula that support teaching and student learning, and has been a member of organizing committees for local, national, and international conferences.

Mary Wilson

Director of the Centre for Academic Excellence at Niagara College. She holds a Doctorate in Education from OISE/UT and is interested in the history of post-secondary curriculum development, and the theory and practice of post-secondary curriculum reform. She values conferences as a rich source of professional learning.

Introduction

Celia Popovic

1 Introduction

This is a book for people who attend conferences, for those who present and for those who organize conferences. All three of these categories may apply to you. The authors are educational developers who are actively involved in supporting research into teaching and learning in universities in the UK and Canada. Their focus is understandably on educational development but the advice is generic and may be applied to any academic conference. That said there are disciplinary differences and cultural distinctions that do need to be considered. For example, in some disciplines it is considered reasonable to be highly critical when work is presented, while in others the expectation is that the community is developmental and supportive.

2 Outline of the Book

The book is presented in three sections. Part 1 focuses on conferences from the perspective of the participant. Chapter 1 offers issues to consider before attending. We ask why anyone would attend a conference given the costs and effort involved. We offer several reasons in part to persuade the reader but also to offer ammunition for anyone who needs to persuade their manager or senior administration that it is a good idea to attend. We go on to offer suggestions on gaining funding to attend. We finish the chapter with some guidance on preparing to attend.

Chapter 2 focuses on effective approaches to take while attending a conference. We offer some advice on note taking and networking, and guidance on selecting between the shiny new but impractical, and those ideas that may be easily implemented at your own institution.

In Chapter 3 we suggest ways to capitalize on the experience of attending a conference when back at the home institution. We discuss how you can use the new ideas you discovered, make use of the contacts formed through networking and share your learning with colleagues.

Part 2 looks at conferences from the perspective of the presenter. Chapter 4 describes the process involved in writing and submitting a successful proposal. We share tips and tricks that have proved effective in producing winning proposals that meet the criteria of the selection committee.

In Chapter 5 there are ideas and suggestions for professional, mesmerising and memorable conference presentations. We provide guidance based on personal experiences of presenting many conference sessions as well as the wisdom gleaned from observing others. This advice includes preparation for your performance at the conference – the best way to present a session, and what will make it memorable and effective.

Chapter 6 explores ways to give an effective keynote presentation While being asked to present a keynote is an honour, not everyone does this well. This chapter is invaluable to anyone who has been asked to give a keynote, but will also be useful for conference organizers wondering how to support a novice keynote speaker.

Part 3 looks at conferences from the perspective of the conference organizer.

The first chapter in this section provides an overview of conference structure, including alternative formats, and ways to decide conference themes. In the second chapter we hone in on a range of session formats, suggesting varied approaches to determine the content of the conference. This includes the means to provide networking opportunities and ways to take advantage of the conference venue.

In Chapter 9 we turn our attention to the impact that conferences might have at a local, regional or national level. The authors share their experiences of impact arising from a decade of co-hosting an annual conference with an institution in another country. They offer suggestions on now to extend the impact of a conference beyond the event itself.

In Chapter 10 we offer guidance on making effective use of social media in conferences.

We conclude in Chapter 11 with guidance on using evaluation of a conference to inform the development and design of future conferences. Whether this is an institutional conference or one run by a committee on behalf of a professional organization we urge you to think about the feedback that will be most helpful in improving year on year, and how to respond to comments.

3   Who Will Find This Book Useful?

This book is written by educational developers, several of whom also identify as belonging to a disciplinary area in addition to educational development. The anticipated audience is much wider than those involved in educational development. This will include:

– Attendees – the first section of the book examines learning as a participant in a conference;
– Presenters – both novice and seasoned will find advice and guidance which will improve the acceptance rate of proposals and enhance their performance;
– Conference organizers – whether this is a local, national or international conference, organizers will benefit from considering their event through the perspectives of the various stakeholders;
– Administrators and senior managers – conference expenditure is a significant budget item for many departments, the advice provided here will help in ensuring effective use of scarce resources.

Acknowledgements

Particular thanks to Mandy Frake-Mistak, our reviewer, and to those who provided anecdotes: Dorothy Missingham, Mandy Frake-Mistak, Bob Parson, and Gary Poole. Also, a very big thank you to our illustrator Millie Popovic.
   Finally, I would like to acknowledge the support and guidance from Nicola Simmons, without whom this book would not have seen the light of day.

5   Underpinning Research

In many of the chapters in this book there is reference to various research projects. The starting point for this book was a research project conducted by Celia Popovic and Fiona Campbell. In 2011 we surveyed participants at several institution and national conferences. We received 178 responses.
   The central question for the research was:

   Does participation in Academic Development conferences impact participants' individual or institutional academic practice?

There were six sub questions:

1. What aspects of conferences make a difference to individuals' academic practice? The content of sessions, the nature of the delivery, the style of presenters, or the contribution of other participants?
2. Which aspects resulted in changes in practice, i.e. participants' individual approach in teaching and learning?
3. Do these changes have an effect on the institutional level?
4. How important is networking?
5. What lasting collaborations have resulted from participation in the conferences?
6. What are the 'best practices' for conferences in the field of Academic Development?

The research project received ethics approval from both home institutions (Edinburgh Napier and York Universities).

The findings from this research are referenced throughout the book.

6   Why Crows?

There's a conference of crows,
called on the coconut tree;
Their rough and raucous cries,
reek of rank acrimony.

Startled by a cuckoo call,
they flap their wings and crow;
The leader, with his beady eyes,
squawks louder and some more...
They congregate each morning,
Here's the lesson to be learned –
When you cannot reach consensus,
The meeting is adjourned...
    Roann Mendriq
    (from http://www.poemhunter.com/poem/conference-of-crows/)

When Fiona Campbell and I first discussed the idea of writing a book on this topic one of us (I shall admit it was me, Celia) was under the mistaken impression that the collective noun for crows was a conference. Running ahead with this idea without checking its veracity I asked my daughter Millie to draw some illustrations for the book. Fiona rather wisely investigated and discovered there is no such thing as a 'conference of crows'. Happily, the wonderful Nicola Simmons came to the rescue with this rather apposite poem. Crisis averted. However, when Alice Cassidy saw Millie's images she pointed out that what Millie had drawn was a specific type of crow (in the Corvid family of crows and their allies; see https://en.wikipedia.org/wiki/Corvidae), known as a rook – common in the UK but not the Americas. So what we thought was a universal symbol turned out to be culturally or geographically specific.

This interchange of information, sharing of ideas and collective knowledge checking is a perfect analogy for many people's experiences at conferences. We attend conferences to learn, but also to share our understanding. In doing so we may discover errors in our thinking, find new areas to explore and ultimately learn from each other. We hope the information, observation and guidance contained in these pages will help to ensure you get the most out of conferences as participant, presenter or organizer.

PART 1

Attending a Conference

∴

CHAPTER 1

Before the Conference

Celia Popovic

In 2010 I visited Canada to attend a conference held by the EDC (Educational Developers Caucus) in Kamloops BC. At the time I was head of an educational development unit in the UK. As a result of a casual conversation with a fellow attendee I heard about a job opening at a university in Toronto. Some 18 months later this resulted in a move of 3,000 miles and a huge change to my career and personal life. Had I not attended the conference I would not have heard about the position. While this is just my experience, many conference participants have similar stories of ways in which contacts made at conferences have had future impact, perhaps with less dramatic outcomes than mine.

1 Introduction

Whether you are planning to attend your first conference or you are a seasoned participant, we provide you with tips and insights that will enable you to get the most out of the experience. Few of us have unlimited funds or time to attend conferences, so we want to make the most of those we can attend. Conferences are expensive in terms of budget but also in time and effort. When you factor in the journey, especially if it is held in a distant location, this can result in significant time away from the home institution. Many universities insist on a participant having a paper accepted at the conference before they will fund attendance. It takes time and effort to create a proposal. In this chapter, you will find the reasons why attending conferences can and should be a good use

© KONINKLIJKE BRILL NV, LEIDEN, 2018 | DOI 10.1163/9789004373013_001

of time and budget. In Chapter 2 we look in detail at ways to make the most of the time spent at a conference, then in Chapter 3 we explore how to maximise the benefits of having attended a conference months or even years later.

2   Why Do People Attend Academic Conferences?

Quotations throughout this chapter come from a research project conducted by Celia Popovic and Fiona Campbell; see the Introduction for further details.

> While at these conferences and for the following weeks, I am usually in a very creative state of mind. Rejuvenated by new ideas and perspectives, some of the most significant changes to my work or programming occur right after my return from a conference.

People have multiple reasons for attending academic conferences. In our research Fiona Campbell and I found that most people say that they are reinvigorated by attending a conference as it provides the opportunity to step away from the every-day, listen to others' work and reflect on their own. Other people are motivated to attend conferences in order to share their work, perhaps to establish their identity in a field or simply to network with others. In our research, we found these were the key reasons people give for attending conferences:

– To make time and space to reflect on practice
– To find out what others are doing
– To update practice and knowledge
– To network with others
– To disseminate one's own work
– To make a name for oneself in the field

2.1   *To Make Time and Space to Reflect on Practice*

> We are all overworked so there is not a lot of time to reflect.

> These kinds of networking interactions help sustain me, both in the field and in my professional life.

> It is always reassuring to know that I am not alone in my role-related issues and that there are others available that I can call upon for further and future discussions around particular issues.

Most people's daily lives are busy with demands. Whether it is juggling home and work, meeting external deadlines or simply keeping on top of email and the expectations of colleagues it can be difficult to find time for reflection. However, as research into the importance of active learning has demonstrated (Kolb, 1984; Di Stefano et al., 2016; Dewey, 1938) reflection is a vital component of learning. Schön's seminal work on the reflective practitioner (Schon, 1983, 1987) suggests that we function more efficiently if we carve out time and space to reflect on what is working and why. Ghaye (2010) argues that the values of reflective practice are a requirement for human flourishing. He refers to the research of Robertson and Cooper (2008), which shows the importance for our wellbeing to have meaning and a sense of purpose in our life and work. Ghaye (2010) argues that reflective practice can help to enhance our wellbeing by providing the opportunity to identify the meaning and sense of purpose in our work. Conferences can provide the space for this reflection. While it may not be necessary to travel to another town or even country in order to stop work and reflect, a conference can be seen as providing permission to do so. A break in the daily routine combined with the influx of new ideas and conversations with new people, or catching up with old acquaintances can provide the stimulus to change habits, question taken for granted assumptions, and identify issues to tackle on return to the normal routine.

While Lewin's (1947) influential work on unfreezing, changing, and freezing is primarily focused on group dynamics, the model works well when applied to an individual. We tend to settle into habits and ways of thinking which have evolved over time and are subject to our experiences. Change can be difficult to enact unless we 'unfreeze' first. This unfreezing involves overcoming inertia and accustomed ways of thinking. Once the change has occurred, and that is rarely without discomfort, then the new way of thinking or behaving has to become habitual. This third phase Lewin calls 'freezing'. For an individual seeking to find new ways to engage in their profession, attendance at a conference may help to bring about the unfreezing as they give themselves space to reflect, to consider new ideas and to plan ways to enhance their chances of changing their behaviour.

2.2   *To Find out What Others Are Doing*

Fantastic examples of high quality resources available.

Made me think differently about what and how we do things at our university and what I can do to change the situation.

Other institutions have tackled problems we are currently chewing over.

Sharing good news stories and learning what other universities are doing in key areas.

The aim of most conferences is to provide a platform for the sharing of knowledge. Most often this is in the form of reporting on research findings. In some fields, it is customary for presenters to share their work by reading a paper. In others, as we will see in Parts 2 and 3 of this book, the format is more interactive. Some conferences make effective use of posters to enable multiple presenters to share their work. Regardless of the medium, conferences provide the opportunity for participants to hear about cutting edge research findings, to get an idea of coming trends, and possibly to identify potential collaborators for future work. The quotations above illustrate the value of hearing from others.

When considering which conference to attend pay attention to the themes of the conference (see Chapter 4), the key note speakers and, if the schedule has been published, the presenters. Ask yourself whether it is likely that this combination of presenters is likely to enable you to expand your knowledge on a given topic.

2.3   *To Update Practice and Knowledge*

We heard and saw real stories, which was very powerful.

This session focused on a research area that is new, exciting and that pushes the boundaries of our understanding

Clear presentation of a dilemma we face at my institution too and a practical demonstration on how they solved that dilemma. I could immediately see how to apply it at my own institution.

This session had a major impact on my professional development.

Some conferences are more effective than others at providing the opportunity to home one's skills and knowledge. Publishers and private companies may take the opportunity to present their latest products during coffee and lunch breaks. These can be valuable opportunities to try out a new resource, to identify a possible publisher for your own work, or discover the solution to a problem you did not know you had.

2.4   *To Network with Others*

Networking is one of the most beneficial aspects of conference attendance and enables what conferences are all about: to confer. As Jeannie Holstein (2013) advises, conferences are:

a vital part of joining the conversation of your peers…and a good way to identify your fellow academic travelers.

As a participant, you will learn so much from these conversations and the experiences and mutual interests you discover. Networking also enables future learning as it may be the foundation for collaborations or partnerships, shared projects and professional conversations you engage in later.

Kevin Fong (2013) suggests the best parts of any conference are the opportunities provided by the coffee break when:

the coffee and the conference programme, it turns out, are just props.

He goes on to say of networking:

What you are really looking for is the chance to chat freely with people you actually want to talk to about stuff that you actually care about. At least, that's the idea.

This is reflected in Nicola Simmons' (2010) blog too where she reflects on the highlights of a conference being the beer and discussion shared with one delegate and the lunch and discussion she shared with another.

The importance of networking was confirmed in our research as 93% of all the respondents surveyed were positive about networking. The comments included:

Extremely useful. Networking is the most essential part of any conference.

These kind of networking interactions help sustain me, both in the field and in my professional life.

Respondents also indicated that they would find it easier to contact colleagues who they had met at a conference rather than 'cold calling' them. The initial contact made at the conference made it easier to follow up on ideas gained, plans devised and advice received there.

The benefits which you can reap as a conference participant from networking were listed by our survey respondents were:

a Meeting and talking to others
b Benefiting from opportunities
c Sharing

a   Meeting and Talking to Others

Networking opportunities provided our survey respondents with the means to meet and talk with new colleagues, reconnect with known colleagues and put a face to a name they knew.

> Always reassuring to know that I am not alone in my role-related issues and there are others available that I can call on for further and future discussions around particular issues.

> If it is not about what you know but who you know, then conferences certainly help me to know who to ask about all sorts of things in my day-to-day academic life.

Meet and Talk to New People; Meet International Colleagues

> Made new contacts who I have now added to my professional social media profiles. This will help me to keep abreast of latest developments, and for others to see my interests.

Meet and Reconnect with Friends and Colleagues from Other Institutions

> Always really useful to renew acquaintances and build new ones.

> Enjoyable, thought-provoking conversations.

Meet and Reconnect with Friends and Colleagues within an Institution

> Great opportunity to meet staff from the wider university outside my immediate school.

> One of the few occasions I get to meet and talk to colleagues from other campuses which I'm not usually able to do.

> As a professional services member of staff, it's a time to meet a wide range of academic staff which I don't often have the opportunity to do.

Put Face to a Name

> Met people face-to-face who I only have spoken previously to virtually.

I was able to make connections with people I am studying with on an online course and to get to know others I am already working with on a cross-institutional course.

b Benefiting from Opportunities

Respondents listed a number of beneficial professional opportunities which resulted from networking including career, collaboration and community.

Career

I'm looking for a new future.

Identified candidates for a post doc fellowship.

As a result of connecting with someone I have been invited to be on a panel for… How cool is that:)

Learnt about the academy.

If you are presenting at a conference, networking also provides a wider audience for your contribution than just those who attended your session as you can also receive valuable and genuine feedback from those who did attend in more informal settings than the session itself.

Collaboration and Community

Networking provides the opportunity to consider collaborating in future in research or academic development, on projects, publications or for funding and grants – or all of these! At the events we surveyed we learned from respondents that invitations were proffered and accepted to be a guest speaker or to facilitate an event or online session for another institution.

Great to network with others who can see the value of a particular theory that could lead to some collaborative work in the future.

Made contact with a possible collaborator for future work.

Made many connections that will hopefully be continued over Twitter and LinkedIn.

Discussions with other participants led to new ideas…for my practice.

Made concrete plans to work together.

I am looking forward to developing these networks further.

Networking also enabled community, as respondents reported that as a result of this they had set up an action learning set, a writing group, a community of practice or mentoring relationships. Also, and significantly, peer discussions brought a 'sense of community'.

Academic work can be so solitary and isolating that it is good to know there are members of the professional community who do what you do.

I met someone who is also a novice and we're going to form a community of practice to help us develop and research our common interests.

We were all facing the same challenge. All keen to explore the issues.

Chance to talk about what is really important rather than what is on the agenda.

c Sharing

Respondents also advised that networking enabled sharing. This sharing included interests, ideas, and approaches, professional experiences, dilemmas and solutions, contacts, networks, research instruments, teaching tools and resources.

Speaking to like-minded people with shared interests

Sharing of thoughts and new knowledge.

I've met people I can continue discussing ideas with.

Finding out who's doing what, where.

Sharing good news stories and learning what other universities are doing in key areas.

Michael Earnst (2004) suggests that the primary reason for attending conferences is that it is a professionally rewarding experience. Not only do you hear the talks that are scheduled, but there is the opportunity to talk with people in corridors and during breaks, people you would not otherwise meet.

Networking with colleagues is frequently cited as the main reason for attending a conference. Some conferences are one-off events run around a specific issue. However, it is more often the case that institutions or professional bodies run annual or biannual events. These conferences may build up a loyal following over time. Those who attend regularly become part of a community. That community is valuable to those who feel they belong but may seem off putting or cliquey to those who are newcomers. In Chapter 2 we explore some techniques to help the novice conference attender feel part of the in crowd quickly and easily.

Networking brings multiple benefits. While institutions may feel pressure to compete with each other for government and research body funding, most academics feel more of an affinity with their discipline than with their institution (Cummings & Finkelstein, 2011). For example, a Biology professor may feel he or she has more in common with a Biology professor from another institution than with an English professor from their own. Conferences provide the opportunity to meet with members of the community beyond those in your own institution. This meeting over mutually shared interest is more likely to result in collaboration in the future. Despite the advantages of technology, our research supported by Salmon (2011) suggests some of us are more likely to work together with someone we have met in person than one we have only ever conversed with online.

2.5   *To Disseminate One's Work*

If conferences are primarily a source of information about other people's work, they are also a platform to disseminate your own findings. See Part 2 for in depth discussion of presenting at conferences. As with any form of communication it is important to identify the most appropriate medium for your presentation. Which conference is the most appropriate will depend on numerous factors, including which one you are able to attend, location, cost, likely participants and so forth. For many of us making a presentation at a conference is a prerequisite for funding. There is a logic to this, if an institution is going to invest in your attendance then they will wish to be assured of a return on that investment. See Chapter 3 for guidance on sharing that knowledge when you return.

While it is usual for participants at a conference to present, this is not always the case; in any event you are unlikely to be presenting on all aspects of your work. Before you attend think about how you can frame your research in a way that is both interesting and engaging for a listener. Practice your 'elevator pitch' – imagine that you have just the time of an elevator ride to say the 10th floor of a building to engage someone in a way that will hook their attention and give them the essence of your area of interest. Dissemination is not confined to scheduled sessions. You may find you engage in numerous discussions of this kind that do not appear to go anywhere, but if you miss the opportunity to connect you may never know that it was there. A great deal of research and successful funding bids emerge from collaborations. Chance discussions and sharing of ideas are at the catalyst of many such serendipitous connections.

2.5.1   To Make a Name for Oneself
One of our research participants said:

> I made new contacts who I have now added to my professional social media profiles (and they have requested to be added). This will help me keep abreast of latest developments and for others to see my interests.

How is it that some people in a field seem to become almost a household name while others are barely recognized? One way to raise your profile is to attend key conferences in your field and become known as someone who is part of that particular crowd. I once asked a highly successful female senior administrator for advice as a woman trying to succeed in a male dominated sector. One key piece of advice she shared was to be sure to ask a question at any public event such as a conference. She said it was not enough to ask a relevant thought provoking question, it was also vital to be sure to state your name and institution as well. Not everyone is comfortable with the idea of self-promotion. However, if you are seeking ways to become part of a community this can be relatively easy way to raise your profile. That said, be careful to ensure that people remember you for positive reasons, such as that is the person who asked that insightful question, rather than as the person who hogged the limelight by making an off-topic observation!

When preparing to attend a conference, think about the image you wish to present to the world. What aspect of your work is likely to be of most value to others? Even if you are at an early stage in your career, perhaps presenting on research for a doctorate, it is likely that you are an expert in your field. You may have spent more time thinking and writing about your particular area of interest than other participants, more than most at least. You can use this to your advantage when trying to make a name for yourself. Become known as the person who knows all there is to know about X. Be generous with your sources and resources, encourage others to think of you first in connection with the particular topic. As time goes on you may find your interests widen or even diverge from your original focus. Be sure to present on these new areas at subsequent conferences if this is the case, so that you can demonstrate your versatility and breadth of interests.

3   How to Get Funding for Conferences

Conferences are not cheap. The most obvious source of funding is your institution. However, there is often competition for limited resources, so what techniques are most likely to work?

Firstly, plan your conference attendance months or even years in advance. Do your research: find out which conferences are most likely to provide the best return on your investment. If your institution requires you to present a paper or run a workshop in order to be funded to attend, this is particularly important. What is your aim in attending? It may be to find the widest audience for your presentation, or perhaps you want to learn about a specific topic, or maybe you wish to increase your network of colleagues. As we have discussed earlier, you may have multiple aims. Once you have an idea of what you want to achieve, you are more likely to be able to choose the most appropriate conference or conferences.

Many conferences are annual or bi-annual events. These conferences often select a different location each time. If travel costs are prohibitive one year, look at the planned locations, it may be scheduled for a closer location in the future. Perhaps it would be better to plan to attend a year later and conserve funds than attend sooner and use up all your reserves. It may be possible to plan a multi-purpose trip around a conference in a particular location. One year I arranged a series of paid workshops at universities in the country where the conference was being held. While this involved a lot of work, the honoraria helped fund the trip. Without them I would not have been able to attend the conference.

When researching a conference start by considering the theme or themes. This should provide a guide to the likely content. The final content of the conference obviously cannot be confirmed until proposals have been selected, so examine the themes closely. If possible, look at the details of previous conferences if this is a regular event. Who is the keynote speaker, or speakers? Are these people you particularly want to hear speak? Is there a link between the speaker or the themes and your current and future work? Have any of your colleagues or friends heard the keynote speaker in the past? If so, ask them how they rated them as speakers. Use your research skills to find out all that you can about the conference if it has been held in the past and the proposed speakers. Many conferences publish conference proceedings both in hard copy and increasingly online.

Put together a case that indicates the reasons why this particular conference is perfect for your needs. Remember to think about the needs of your department or institution and the potential benefit to whoever foots the bill. Even if you have autonomy over your conference budget, this can be useful to help you decide whether this really is a good conference for you to attend, If, like many of us, someone else will ultimately decide whether you can go, this is invaluable. You may wish to consider writing a letter to whoever approves the expense claim explaining in detail the benefits that would accrue both to you and your institution if you attend.

Depending on your situation there may be bursaries provided by the organization behind the conference, check if you are eligible and if so apply. Read the small print, some organizations offer preferential rates to those who volunteer to assist in the running of the conference. If you are able to volunteer then do so.

Ask your contacts if they know of any funds and whether they have had success in getting funding. They may know of funds that were not applicable to them but could be appropriate for you.

4   Preparing to Attend a Conference

Ask yourself what you want to get out of the conference. Why are you attending? Perhaps some of your motivators have been discussed above; perhaps you have some specific outcomes in mind. What are they?

4.1   *Make Your Travel Plans*
Although some bargain flights may be offered close to the time of travel, this is not the time to gamble. Large conferences often result in sell outs of hotels and flights.

The conference website will tell you when the conference begins and ends. Check if there will be any pre-conference events. It may seem obvious to suggest that you book your travel to allow you to attend the whole conference but it is surprising the number of people who miss the start or end of the conference. Having made the investment of time and money in attending you will wish to get the most return. Allow time for transfers from the conference venue to the airport or station as appropriate.

Use any communication means provided to reach out to others to see if you can share taxis or car pool as appropriate. It is not unusual for several people to arrive at train station or airport at the same time for the same conference but not share taxis to the venue because they are unaware of each other. It is of course easier to arrange taxi shares at the end of the conference.

Check your documentation is in order. If you are travelling to another country be sure to ensure your passport is valid and that you meet any visa requirements. It is often necessary to have a passport that is valid for 6 months beyond the intended visit, so be sure to check this in good time.

One year I was due to attend a conference in Seattle and had arranged for my husband to accompany me. We thought we would take the opportunity to stay on for a few days after the conference. It is not difficult to imagine the conversation that took place between us when it transpired that while my husband's passport was valid it was due to expire before the time required by the US customs and immigration department. Needless to say, I still attended the conference but we didn't take the short vacation afterwards!

4.2 *Book Accommodation*

Some conferences include accommodation in the conference price; most do not. When booking accommodation use Google maps (or a similar app) or ask for advice about the distance from the accommodation to the venue. Depending on location and time of year this could be critical. A 20 minute walk to the venue might be attractive if the weather is kind, but mid-winter in a Canadian city might be quite a different proposition, as I discovered at an EDC conference held in February in Winnipeg, for instance.

Most hotels will accept a booking without requiring a deposit. Book early if this is the case as it is not unusual for the conference hotel to sell out of rooms. Other hotels are most likely available but will be less convenient than the one where the conference is held. While you will wish to wait for confirmation that your proposal has been accepted, for any non-refundable expenses such as flights, book your hotel room immediately. Make a note of the cancellation policy and if necessary ensure you cancel in good time.

As with taxi shares if you are willing to share accommodation to reduce costs refer to the participant list to see if there is anyone you know who may appreciate the offer to share a room. Air BnB offers an economical alternative to conventional hotels as do Bed and Breakfast providers. Some conferences, particularly those held at colleges and universities offer student accommodation (residence) which can be significantly less expensive than mainstream hotels. And it is a great way to network!

Take a look at the conference website as this is likely to contain information about accommodation, things to see, places to eat in the area and often much more.

4.3 *Read the Schedule*

Review the schedule carefully. In most conferences there are multiple sessions. If you are presenting at the conference, first ensure you know the date and time of your own session. See Part 2 for more detailed advice and guidance about preparing your presentation.

Most conferences require participants to make choices. You may be required to announce your selections ahead of the conference, but even if this is not the case it is wise to read the schedule in advance and at least start to make your selections. If you find that you would like to attend multiple sessions you will feel less stressed and will be more likely to make the best decision if you have prepared ahead of time. Be aware that there may be last minute changes, resulting in sessions being cancelled. In this case it may be helpful to know that there is an alternate that you are interested in attending. As we will discuss in Part 2, it is also possible to elect not to attend a session.

A read through the schedule will help you to identify the key themes of the conference. Often these are multiple, and the conference organizers build the schedule such that it is possible to follow a particular theme or move between multiple themes. When you attend you may find yourself in the room with the same people repeatedly, particularly if you follow a particular theme. These may be ideal candidates for you to build into your network since you clearly have this interest in common.

4.4   *Identify People You Wish to Meet*

You may have a broad sense of the people you would like to meet at the conference. For example, others in a similar role or career stage, potential mentors or key figures in your field. You may have a more specific list in mind of people you would like to get to know such as well-regarded authors or researchers.

If it is available, view the participant list before you attend the conference. Highlight names of those you know you would like to meet. If appropriate you may consider emailing them before the conference to say how delighted you are to see that you are both attending the same event and that you hope to chat with them at the conference. If this is a cold call, in other words this email is the first contact you have had with the recipient, you may wish to include a reason why the other person might be as keen as you to make contact. Perhaps you have a shared research interest, for example.

4.5   *Pack Your Bags*

So now you are ready to pack your case – you have booked your travel, secured your accommodation and registered for the conference. Now what? For a somewhat light-hearted but practical guide to what to pack see Tara Siebarth's blog for University Affairs at http://www.universityaffairs.ca/career-advice/ careers-cafe/what-to-pack-for-an-academic-conference/.

Tara suggests the following:

1   Travel light – if possible avoid checking baggage on flights. Tara suggests

taking a roller suitcase and a back pack. The suitcase is considered a standard item by most airlines – and 'should not exceed the following measurements: 21 inches × 9 inches × 15 inches, and should not weigh more than 20 pounds'. The metric equivalent of this is 53cm × 23cm × 38cm, weight 9kg.

2 Take clothing that is both smart and comfortable. Take comfortable shoes and clothes that can be easily mixed and matched. Sticking to a simple colour palette usually means you can take fewer items. Be aware that rooms may be overheated in the winter and overly cooled in the summer so bring clothes that can be layered.

3 Visit OneBag.com for detailed advice on travelling light.

Having read the schedule, you will know if there is a conference dinner. If this is optional and you are on a tight budget, you may question whether or not to attend. There are advantages in attending, aside from the quality of the food and entertainment on offer. The opportunity to network is the primary benefit. However, most dinners are structured such that diners are allocated to join a random table group, offering limited opportunities to chat with others. If this is a conference that tends to build community, for example an annual gathering of a professional body, you would be well advised to attend. As with the conference itself, weigh up the pros and cons of attending including the financial cost and professional opportunities before deciding. If you do choose to attend, be sure to include appropriate clothing for the event in your packing.

Aside from clothes and personal items, make sure you pack all you will need for your presentation. Are you expected to bring a lap top for example, or will this be provided? For peace of mind take more than one version of your presentation; for instance, saved on a laptop and on a memory stick kept in a separate location, or uploaded to the internet. See Chapter 5 for detailed guidance on preparing to give a presentation.

4.6   *Dealing with Expenses*

Make sure you are familiar with any terms associated with your funding. Some universities, for instance, require the production of proof of travel. You may be required to provide a copy of a boarding card, for instance. Find out beforehand and be sure to keep all receipts and other documents ready for your return. One practical suggestion is to use a zip lock bag to collect your receipts.

4.7   *Summary*

In this chapter, we reviewed the reasons why in an age of social media many of us continue to attend conferences. There are several reasons, but the key is in the value of face to face interaction. When tens, or even hundreds of people congregate in the same space with a common interest, magical things can happen. Connections are made, relationships are reinforced; as ideas percolate and learning is shared, knowledge is disseminated and created. In the same way that we learn more as a member of a group of learners in a class, we learn more as professionals when we meet in person and share our thoughts and ideas over mundane activities such as eating and drinking. Conferences are expensive in terms of resource including time, and not all are equally valuable. We explored in this chapter, aspects to consider when deciding whether or not to attend a particular conference. We concluded with considerations of actions to take before attending. In the next chapter we discuss how to get the most out of a conference while you are there.

References

Cummings, W. K., & Finkelstein, M. J. (2011). Declining institutional loyalty. *Scholars in the Changing American Academy*, *4*, 131–140. Retrieved August, 2016, from http://link.springer.com/chapter/10.1007/978-94-007-2730-4_9/fulltext.html

Dewey, J. (1938). *Experience and education*. New York, NY: Kappa Delta Pi.

Di Stefano, G., Gino, F., Pisano, G. P., & Staats, B. R. (2016). *Making experience count: The role of reflection in individual learning* (Harvard Business School NOM Unit, Working Paper No. 14–093). Retrieved August, 2016, from http://papers.ssrn.com/sol3/papers.cfm?abstract_id=2414478

Earnst, M. (2004). *Attending and academic conference*. Retrieved August, 2016, from https://homes.cs.washington.edu/~mernst/advice/conference-attendance.html

Fong, K. (2013). The unconference call: Opinion. *The Times Higher Education Supplement*, No. 2121, October 3.

Ghaye, T. (2010). *Teaching and learning through reflective practice: A practical guide for positive action*. London: Routledge.

Holstein, J. (2013, September 26). How to make the most of academic conferences, five tips. *The Guardian*. Retrieved from https://www.theguardian.com/higher-education-network/blog/2013/sep/26/academic-conference-five-tips-research

Kolb, D. A. (1984). *Experimental learning: Experience as the source of learning and development*. Englewood Cliffs, NJ: Prentice-Hall.

Lewin, K. (1947, June). Frontiers in group dynamics. *Human Relations, 1*, 5–41.

Morison, S. E. (1936). *Harvard college in the seventeenth century*. Cambridge, MA: Harvard University Press.

Robertson, I., & Cooper, C. (2008). *Well-being at work: The new view*. Manchester: Robertson Cooper Ltd.

Salmon, G. (2011). *E-moderating: The key to teaching and learning online* (3rd ed.). New York, NY: Routledge.

Schon, D. (1983). *The reflective practitioner: How professionals think in action.* London: Temple Smith.

Schon, D. (1987). *Educating the reflective practitioner.* San Francisco, CA: Jossey Bass.

Simmons, N. (2010). *Renewing my scholarship: Journeys away* (Centre for Teaching Excellence Blog). Waterloo: University of Waterloo. Retrieved December 30, 2016, from http://cte-blog.uwaterloo.ca/?p=1490

CHAPTER 2

During the Conference

Celia Popovic and Fiona Campbell

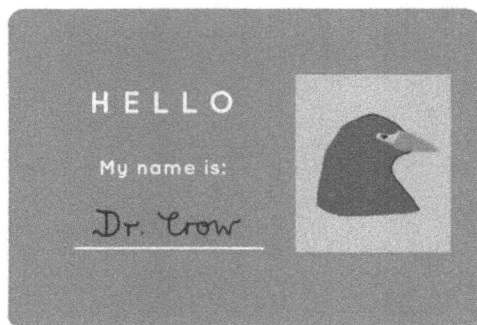

At a conference a few years ago, I heard about a novel approach to recognising good teaching. Full of enthusiasm I attempted to recreate the idea at my home institution. It failed. A year or so later, I was at another conference where I heard another institution had implemented the approach. This second example inspired me further and on my return to my university I tried again. This time it was a success. Conferences can inspire in many ways. In this case it was the original idea supported by an example of a successful application that led to change at my own institution.

1 Introduction

As we established in Chapter 1, conferences are expensive in terms of time and funds. It is important to make the most of the event, while preserving energy and enthusiasm. In this chapter, we provide practical hands on guidance on participating fully, recording your experience, making the most of the opportunities to meet with others and finding ways to apply your experience to your own context.

As we saw in the previous chapter, many conference participants claim networking as their primary reason for attending conferences. In this chapter, we will provide practical suggestions to assist in making the most of potential connections.

© KONINKLIJKE BRILL NV, LEIDEN, 2018 | DOI 10.1163/9789004373013_002

The chapter will also cover how to learn from conferences and, crucially, apply that learning to your own context. We will also explore tactics for ensuring that the new ideas and enthusiasm you return home with does not wane under the pressure of the day to day job, but remains upper most in your thinking.

2 Deciding What to Attend

In deciding to attend a conference, you will have researched the intended aims of the meeting, and may have examined the programme. We will now discuss how to decide which elements of the conference to attend. Many conferences provide alternate or parallel sessions – multiple events running simultaneously. It can be difficult to decide which to attend and which to miss. If you are attending a conference with others from your institution, discuss which sessions you will attend and agree to share notes afterwards of the ones your colleagues were able to join. Having said that, it can be illuminating to attend the same session with a colleague and compare notes afterwards. The resulting discussion can be extremely useful in clarifying misunderstandings, identifying differences of opinions (between colleagues and/or with the presenter), and deciding how to effect change together on your return to base.

When choosing a session, read the schedule carefully. If there are multiple concurrent sessions consider using this technique. Begin by ticking any sessions that strike you as potentially relevant. Strike out any that are definitely not of interest. If there are more than one with a tick, read the abstracts carefully. Sometimes organizers group three or four presentations in the same slot; it may or may not be possible to move between presentations in different rooms. If possible find out where the rooms are located to see if this is feasible. It does depend on the presenters keeping strictly to time, but may solve a problem if there are two that you would like to see taking place at different times within the same session. Having made a decision regarding which session to attend, consider asking the other presenter(s) if they would share their slides with you. If you would like to hear more about their work aim to deliberately strike up a conversation with them over lunch or coffee break.

When you can, stick to the sessions you have chosen. This is courteous to the presenter (who may have limited attendance at their session and your absence will make a hole) and to other participants (who may not have been able to attend this season if it was fully booked. If many participants change their minds after booking a session, it can cause a headache for the organisers with sessions overrun or underpopulated.

Also ensure you turn up to the session on time. We've all been there: got involved in an interesting conversation in the coffee break and not noticed the time slipping away, other participants leaving the room and the sessions starting. But having participants trickle in late can be very off-putting for the presenters and other participants at the session and can play havoc for the session timing and plans. After you leave each session, just remind yourself from the conference programme where you need to be and when so that you are ready to make the move and can benefit from arriving at the session on time and getting the most out of the presentation and discussion.

All too commonly, and hugely frustratingly for participants, some sessions within parallel streams overrun making it difficult to move to a session in another stream. This really comes down to poor time management by the session presenter or chair (if there is one). If this happens to you and you are very keen to attend the other session, just leave as quietly as you can, avoiding disrupting the session. Hopefully your departure – and perhaps that of others – should encourage the presenter to wind up their session enabling the sessions ahead to start.

3   Participating Fully in Sessions

To get the most out of the sessions you attend, you should participate fully. Clearly, this involves being wholly present in the session and not getting distracted by, for instance, work emails that pop up on your phone. Avoid sitting at the back during sessions and listening to a presentation with half an ear. It is worth contributing as much as you feel comfortable: the more you put into the session, the more you will get out of it. Contribute proactively by taking advantage of the interactive opportunities in the sessions to ask questions, learn from others, suggest ideas, ask questions, contribute to discussions and, in the case of workshops, engage enthusiastically in the activities involved. Some of this may feel difficult if you are a new conference participant or believe you are less experienced and more junior than others in the session, but your fresh insights are likely to be very much welcomed. Plus, your question will be as valid and useful as anyone else's, and may, in fact, be the very one that all the other session participants were also wanting to ask.

In asking questions of the presenter, do so politely and clearly. Some questioners at conferences use the opportunity to lay into the presenter and their work or to bring their own pet theory. You may not agree with or like their work, but the question slot at the end of their presentation is not the time to bring them to their knees. This is not helpful to anyone and a more professional approach is to ask genuine questions and so elicit a positive response from the presenter which may help better understand their approach and outcomes.

In engaging in workshop activities, do put aside inhibitions and engage fully. The workshop facilitator is likely to have spent much time designing interactive opportunities which will help you contextualise their work, realise its relevance to yourself. and enable the interchange of ideas between all the participants. So, if something seems a little wacky, give the facilitator the benefit of the doubt and go with the flow. Not only will it be more likely that you will benefit from the session but you may also pick up strategies and tactics for providing presentations and facilitating workshops yourself.

4   Keeping a Record – Note Takng

Some people are content to attend a conference without taking any notes. They listen to the keynotes and presentations and rely on their memory to recall any key issues or thoughts. Most of us, however, benefit from making some kind of record at the time, for future reference.

Matt Heinz (2013) has some practical suggestions based on attending business oriented conferences which translate well to the academic conference. He suggests the following:

- Create a system in advance
- Come prepared with your own tools
- Use a keyboard if possible
- Have a paper or tablet handy for sketching
- Highlight to dos and key points in your note for easy access later
- Name and save files by topic, speaker or session
- Dedicate time to review and process
- Publish or share your notes with your team.

We will look at most of these suggestions in this chapter, but will address the last two, reflection and sharing, in Chapter 3.

4.1   *Note Taking Systems*
Scott Berkun (2014) describes an effective method of taking notes that he calls Min/Max note taking. He reminds us that human memory is fallible, that we remember less than we expect to and that at events such as a conference we are bombarded with information. His advice is paraphrased as follows:

> When the session ends immediately make a note of 5 bullet points. Do this for every session. This may be positive or negative points, it could be questions or comments. The audience for this note is a future you, no

one else. You can use breaks or lunch time to make the notes if you are not able to do it immediately after the session ends. Annotate notes that you make of links or URLs, remind your future self why you thought they might be useful to you. Post your summary on your blog or using social media such as Facebook or Twitter using the conference hashtag. This will encourage others to share their learning, which may well include aspects that did not occur to you.

See Chapter 10 for more advice on using social media in conferences.

Celine Roque (2010) supports some of these suggestions while adding others. She suggests that it is most important to be present and attentive. It makes little sense to be present for a one hour talk for instance and spend the time making notes or talking to the person next to us then to rely on a recording of the session to find out what was said. Take meaningful notes at the time, ask yourself the purpose of the notes you are taking.

Boch and Pialot (2005) report that since the average speed of note taking by students is 0.3 to 0.4 words per second while the average lecturer speaks at around 2 to 3 words per second, it is not possible to record verbatim all that is said. The same is true for conference attendees. Boch and Pialot also indicate the reasons for taking notes is twofold, it is both to record information and aid reflection. You may obtain better recall later if you use a spatial representation of some kind such as a mind map rather than just jot down partial transcript of what was said. See Julia Forsythe's work for more inspiration (http://gforsythe.ca/).

There are many methods of note taking, most of which are designed for students taking notes from lectures. Some of these can be adapted for use in a conference, since in essence a lecture and a conference presentation are so similar as to be indistinct from each other.

One of the most popular, certainly in North America, is the Cornell method (Cornell University, n.d.). This method requires some minor preparation. Rule a vertical line on your note pad. This should be roughly a third of the total width of the page from the left side. This is the cue column. The other larger column is the note taking column. Use short sentences to record key points during the presentation. *As soon after the session as possible* use the cue column to annotate your notes with questions, connections and thoughts provoked by the content. Cover the content column and read the notes in the cue column. Without referring to the content answer your own questions. This process will help to consolidate your understanding and memory of the content. Finally summarise your notes at the bottom of the page, this will be your take away from the session.

The Outline method (Cal Poly, 2016) uses location on the page to indicate levels of importance in relation to the other notes. The major point is recorded on the far left of the page. A subsidiary point is recorded below this indented towards the right. For example:

Before the Conference
   Introduction
   Why do people attend conferences?
   Key reasons why people attend
During the Conference
   Introduction
   Deciding what to attend

With practice, this can be a highly effective method to take notes, but it does rely on the presentation (or lecture) being reasonably well organized in the first place.

Thirdly, the Mapping method (Cal Poly, 2016) is popular with many people, particularly those who prefer a visual representation of information to unbroken text. Ideas are grouped on the page showing their links to other ideas. For example:

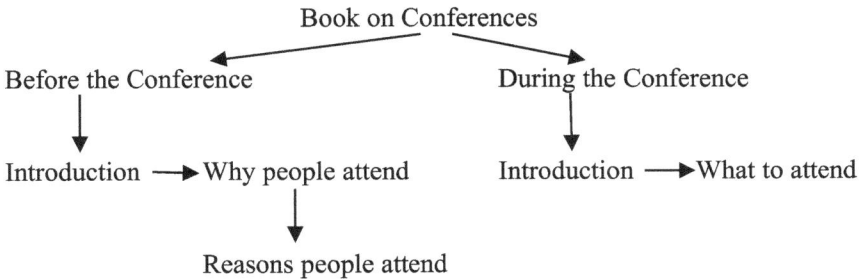

4.4 *Electronic versus Paper*

Do we remember things better if we hand write than if we type them? Melanie Pinola (2011) suggests this may be true. If you do prefer to take notes electronically, find out before you attend the conference whether wifi will be available. While this is increasingly common it may be necessary for you to make your own arrangements with your phone provider. It is not imperative to access the internet to take notes electronically, but there are some methods that require an online presence. Be sure to take your charger and to ensure that you recharge electronic devices each evening of the conference.

Rich Brooks (2013) suggests 10 apps for use at conferences. Some of these are useful for taking notes, or recording your impressions.

Brooks' list:

– Evernote
– Twitter
– Facebook messenger
– Foursquare
– Cardmunch
– Evernote Hello
– Camera App such as Instagram
– Video App such as Andromedia
– Shoeboxed
– Facebook

We will discuss the use of some of these apps in the next section on networking, and in Chapter 10 regarding using social media as a conference designer.

Texter is useful for creating shorthand versions of words, as you take notes you can create a short hand code, for instance CN for conference notes, type CN in place of the full words and later Texter will convert the shorthand version back into the full word(s).

5   How to Network

We have talked about the importance and benefits of networking in Chapter 1, in this section we will suggest ways to go about it. What is the best way to engage in networking and achieve the outcomes you want? If you are new to conferences or this conference in particular, it can seem daunting to find a way into discussions between what appears to be old friends and/or senior professionals. As with any form of social interaction, you really need to take a big breath and just do it – and, when you do, you will be pleasantly surprised by the number of people there who will be interested in talking to you. In fact, they are very likely to be delighted to have the opportunity to talk to someone new rather than the same old folk they have been seeing at the same conferences over the years and they have heard saying much the same many times before. Of course, there will be others – just like you – who are newbies and keen to network too.

To help participants, the conference organiser is likely to have organised a range of different opportunities for informal and formal networking and it is up to you to make the most of these.

5.1   *Wear Your Badge*

Yes, it is as simple as that! Wearing your badge makes introductions easier and will help people remember your name. Wearing your own badge also gives you the opportunity to look at the badges of others and so discover people you were hoping to meet and those you didn't know before but turn out to be interesting, valuable and enjoyable to confer with.

5.2   *Conference Delegate List*

Make this essential reading. We find the delegate list THE single most useful piece of paper at conferences and always spend the first few minutes of a conference quickly scanning the names of those there and their respective institutions and organisations. From the list, you are able to identify new people you would like to meet: those who have written research, papers and books you have read or heard about, or are doing things you are interested in or those you would like the opportunity to work with. Of course, you may also come across people on the list you already know or have come across elsewhere and you can reestablish your acquaintance with them. Once you know who is there, it is easy to find ways to meet them.

One of us, Fiona, once travelled to Stockholm for an international conference to find there was no Delegate List. She says: Imagine my horror! It was so very hard to make connections when I had no idea who was there beyond those I already knew. So, I just decided to bite the bullet and walked up to many strangers, introducing myself and engaging them in conversations. It was a little hit and miss but did result in some beneficial networking. Serendipity can work.

5.3   *Business Cards*

Collect and keep business cards and note when and why you kept a card. This will enable you to follow up more easily after the conference if you want to continue the contact.

In giving your card to others, add information and details to help them to remember you. When you see someone a second or third time remind them what you spoke about or the context of your last encounter.

5.4   *Networking Area*

The conference organisers are likely to designate a specific area of the conference venue for networking. This may be just a small corner of a social area or a specific location designed for this purpose with comfortable seating and coffee and refreshments continuously on tap. Take time to identify the designated area in your conference and visit it often to see who is there that you may want to strike up a conversation with on an area of professional interest.

5.5   Networking Times

Of course, any break, meal or chance meeting is an opportunity for you to network. But the conference programme may well have specific times designated for informal networking. Take advantage of these timetabled sessions as everyone present should be there for the same purpose and some valuable discussions can be had, contacts made and collaborations initiated.

5.6   Networking Events

The conference programme may well also include some activities intended to break the ice between participants and enable and encourage the development of new contacts. These could include a fun means of enabling mutual introductions, or a professional form of speed-dating providing a very short time for interests and activities to be shared or an academic 'marketplace' where participants who have pre-identified their interests can meet like-minded others.

DO participate in these! They are a surprisingly fertile and valuable means of developing professional relationships which can bear fruit through later collaborations.

5.7   A New Delegates' Breakfast or Lunch

Look out for this opportunity as many conferences organise these type of sessions as a way to welcome new participants and to help them navigate the conference. You, together with other new participants, will be encouraged to join members of the conference planning team or the association's executive over a meal. This informal session provides an excellent opportunity for all there to meet each other and share aspirations of the conference. The organisers will be particularly interested in what encouraged you, as a new participant, to participate in the conference and your initial experiences of it, so arrive ready to contribute your views.

5.8   Reception and Conference Dinner

This occasion is a stalwart of conferences and provides an excellent opportunity for you to have in-depth conversations in a convivial atmosphere with those on your table. As discussed in the previous chapter, the benefits of networking at these events may outweigh the costs, if it is optional.

If you are new to the conference, it can be daunting to go into the venue's banqueting suite and see tables already filling with other participants already chatting happily as if to old friends. You can make this easier on yourself by striking up a conversation at the pre-dinner reception with people you would be keen to dine with and then go into dinner with them. But do avoid sitting with colleagues or people you already know well if you can as you will lose out on the opportunity to make new professional relationships and enjoy the company of others.

One of us, Fiona, walked into the banqueting hall where a huge international – and rather intimidating conference dinner was being held – in Barcelona. She says: I steeled myself to walk past tables with known colleagues and friendly faces and sit at a table where I didn't recognise anyone. It turned out to be a table of colleagues from Norwegian institutions. They made me very welcome and spoke for the whole evening in English for my benefit. By the end of the evening, we had found out that we had some similar areas of focus which formed the foundation for later collaborative work – together with a shared interest in malt whiskies! It turned out to be a very enjoyable and memorable evening for me, and all the better for being unanticipated.

And of course, there are often further cordial opportunities after the dinner: perhaps take your coffee to another table so you can chat with other delegates, enjoy a late drink with others in the bar – or make the most of the chance to hit the floor. As Jeannie Holstein (2013) concludes:

> Yes, go to the conference dinner. Sit at a table with interesting people you've just met or don't know. And, of course, don't forget to dance.

6   Learning from Conferences

In this section, we will look at what you can expect to learn from attending conferences based on the responses to the people we surveyed within our research. We will focus on what our respondents told us in terms of:

– Learning from session content
– Learning from session formats and styles

6.1   *Learning from Session Content*

The outcomes from our research showed that, for the respondents surveyed, there was a huge amount of learning. People discussed in their responses – sometimes at some length and in some detail – what they had learned from the sessions. They learned of other people's experiences, of new tools and resources, of new approaches, of different ways they could do the same thing and different ways they could do different things. It was a very long list!

> A fascinating topic, somewhat new to me, with lots of potential. A real treat.

We got a hands-on experience that we could easily take away.

I will seek to use these practices.

Came away with some solid ideas that I can use.

Useful materials shared in the session which can be passed onto other teaching staff within my institution.

Great ideas to take away and put into practice.

Made me think differently about what and how we do things at our university and what I can do to change the situation.

[I will go back and] breathe a little fresh air into our faculty development initiatives.

Likely to inform the university's teaching and learning strategy in the future.

Made me remember why I chose to work in higher education, and gave me hope that there was time yet to achieve what I wanted and that you can always learn!

6.2   *Learning from Session Formats and Styles*
The research also showed how much the respondents had learned from the approach presenters and facilitators took in their sessions and were keen to use the methods they had seen. This included how to encourage participation and interactivity and some were planning to redesign their workshops so that they were more interactive.

Lots of ways the conference will impact – seeing different presentation styles, encountering different workshop activities etc.

This resonates very much with our own experience of conferences which always enable us to return to base with a new way of doing things. A particular example of this is Dialogue Sheets which one of us, Fiona first encountered at a conference in 2008 in a session entitled *Placing student voices at the heart of institutional dialogue facilitated by* Flint and Oxley (2008). She says: I am so glad I chose to attend their session! They introduced Dialogue Sheets in an approach that followed on from the work of Holtham and Courtney (2006) and I was hugely impressed by their benefits as I experienced them in terms of purposefulness, inclusivity and democratisation.

I went on to use Dialogue Sheets myself for strategic discussions, project management and for faculty development and for work focused on technology-enhanced learning, course leadership and academic transitions. Colleagues used them too in exciting ways and in different contexts. With each interaction, we tried something new and evolved our use of them. In 2013, together with colleagues, I brought the Dialogue Sheet approach back to a Staff and Educational Development Association conference showing how we were using them across our institution to engender creative professional conversations around academic leadership (Hanna et al., 2014).

This is an example of how learning gained at a conference has been used and adapted for a range of purposes. The icing on the cake is when you can bring that learning back to a conference setting to allow others to learn from it – and be inspired to take it even further. This is definitely a win, win, win!

7   Applying Learning to Your Context

Once you get back to base – how do you apply all these amazing ideas? This requires cold cool reflection. Chapter 3 looks in more detail at ways to follow up on your learning; here we help you to apply your learning to your own context while still at the conference.

7.1   *Relevance and Feasibility to You and Your Context*
You may come across some brilliant ideas and suggestions, indeed if it is a good conference we would hope that you do. Before leaping to the conclusion that these are things you must immediately implement in your workplace, take some time to reflect on them. Be critical in assessing the relevance of the idea. What was the presenter's context? While universities and colleges share many universal conditions, such as being concerned with teaching and learning, there are multiple variables that can affect the likelihood of being able to apply an idea from one place to another. In some institutions it can be easier to bring in a new idea than in others. A tried and tested idea from another institution may be welcomed in some but rejected in another as not being 'from here'. Also, an approach that works well in a small private college may not be easily implemented in a large research intensive university.

If this is a good idea that may be feasible for your institution ask yourself who is the decision maker who could make this happen. If this is not you, is there someone at your conference from your institution who would benefit from making a contact? For example, one of us, Celia, participated in a conference in South Africa with a colleague. She says: My colleague attended a session without me and realized that the approach that was described in the session had relevance to a project we were both working on. After the session he explained the connection to me and ensured that I met with the presenter. Without this connection being made for me, as the institutional decision maker in this case, I would not have known about the presenter and his work, and the implications for our institution.

Assuming this is a multi-day conference, spend time each evening reflecting back on the presentations and workshops that you attended.

– Make a note of what stood out
– Write a short summary identifying the key themes
– Identify anyone attending the conference who you would like to connect with the following day
– Review any business cards you collected, remind yourself why you took the card. If you did not do so at the time, make a note on the card to remind you of the context. Send a brief email to cement the connection and record a reminder to follow up with the person later.

Take advantage of any opportunities the conference organisers offer to help you to consider applying the learning you have gained after the conference. For instance, you may be asked to decide on one or more significant things that you have learned and are keen to apply to your context. Recording these will be a useful process as it will enable you to begin to think about some of the contextual and implementation issues. You will also have something recorded that you can return to. For instance, the organisers may furnish you with a postcard for you to self-address and to write the ideas down on. Ensure you complete it fully as you will be grateful for the insights and detail you have included when the postcard finds its way to you a month or so hence when you, perhaps now mired in the daily routine. The postcard will prompt you to think back to the ideas which inspired it and can consider again, with renewed enthusiasm, how you can carry them forward to benefit academic practice and, ultimately, the learning experience of students.

8   Evaluating the Conference

You can also make a significant difference to learning from the conference by completing any evaluation or feedback requested. By reflecting on the positive and less positive aspects of the conference and how the content and nature of the conference has contributed to your learning, you will provide the conference organisers with much valuable information. This can be used by them to develop their practice and enhance conference provision in future. It will also help you know what aspects of conference participation and provision you benefit most from and so help you in future when choosing events and sessions. See Chapter 11 for evaluating conferences from an organiser's perspective.

As the conference comes to an end be sure to store your notes, the conference schedule, any handouts, business cards and leaflets that you have collected during the conference. As you make your way home or back to the office, ruminate on the key lessons from the conference and prioritize your steps on returning to work.

References

Berkun, S. (2014). *Min/max note taking for conferences.* Retrieved December 30, 2016, from http://scottberkun.com/2014/min-max-note-taking/

Boch, F., & Piolat, A. (2005). Note taking and learning: A summary of research. *The WAC (Writing Across the Curriculum) Journal, 16*, 101–113.

Brooks, R. (2013). 10 mobile apps no conference attendee should be without. *Social Media Examiner.* Retrieved December 30, 2016, from http://www.socialmediaexaminer.com/10-mobile-apps-for-conferences/

Cal Poly. (2016). *Note taking systems.* Retrieved December 30, 2016, from http://sas.calpoly.edu/asc/ssl/notetakingsystems.html#outline

Cornell University. (n.d.). *The cornell note-taking system.* Retrieved December 30, 2016, from http://lsc.cornell.edu/wp-content/uploads/2015/10/Cornell-NoteTaking-System.pdf

Hanna, B., Campbell, F., & Mowat, E. (2014). *Enabling creative professional conversations around academic leadership through dialogue.* Educational Developments 15.3 Staff and Educational Development Association.

Heinz, M. (2013). *How to take great notes at a conference.* Retrieved December 30, 2016, from https://www.salesforce.com/blog/2013/11/note-taking-tips-gp.html

Holtham, C., & Courtney, N. (2006). About dialogue sheets. *Quality in Business Education.* Retrieved from http://www.qube.ac.uk/QuBE/toolbox/diags/dialogsheet/dialsht/

Oxley, A., & Flint, A. (2008). Placing student voices at the heart of institutional dialogue. *Educational Developments, 9*(3), 14–16.

Pinola, M. (2011). Why you learn more effectively by writing than by typing. *Life Hacker.* Retrieved December 30, 2016, from http://lifehacker.com/5738093/why-you-learn-more-effectively-by-writing-than-by-typing

Roque, C. (2010). *How to take effective conference notes.* Retrieved December 30, 2016, from https://gigaom.com/2010/09/06/how-to-take-effective-conference-notes/

CHAPTER 3

After the Conference

Celia Popovic

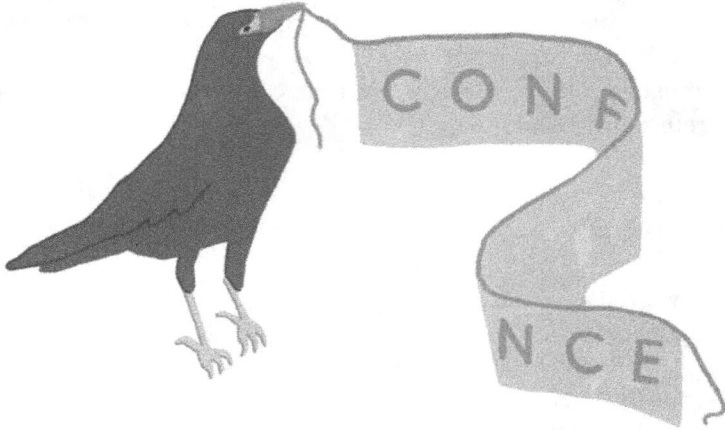

Reflecting back on a conference held at my own institution some years ago, I realised in hindsight that themes can emerge during the conference that may not be the ones intended by the organizers. Sometimes those emergent themes are not obvious in individual sessions but become clear in reflection. When looking back over my notes and sharing impressions with colleagues, it became clear that the main take away from colleagues was a desire to build community. This was not a key theme of the conference, which had been focused on improving student learning. Building community has an impact on student learning, but more specifically the concern was over the perceived lack of community shared by instructors. This was not something that emerged from the conference evaluation, it was an impression that came from reviewing our individual responses to conference sessions. As a result of this observation I made sure to address this theme in a future conference.

1 Introduction

Practices and procedures tend to focus on the lead up to a conference and the event itself with little said about the aftermath. This is odd given that

© KONINKLIJKE BRILL NV, LEIDEN, 2018 | DOI 10.1163/9789004373013_003

conferences seem pretty pointless unless they lead to some future action. Whether that is a change in practice that can be directly attributed to the conference, or a partnership that comes from a conference encounter, or perhaps the slow emergence of a new idea or approach sparked by an event at a conference, these changes are the reason for attending. Consequently, I focus here on actions and approaches that can be taken once we return from a conference, which are designed to maximize the potential benefits of attending.

This chapter begins by reflecting on the use of the notes taken at the conference, including how to make use of those notes, and experiences. There follows practical advice and suggestions concerning cementing contacts made in networking sessions, lunches, dinners and chance encounters. The chapter concludes with reflections on learning and considering what next. Some of the future actions may involve presenting at a conference, in which case Part 2 will be of interest to you, or you may plan to host your own conference, if so you are encouraged to dip into Part 3.

2   Reviewing Notes and Experiences

Once you return to your day to day life it is easy to put all the learning from the conference out of mind. Instead review your notes as soon after you return from the conference as you can. The temptation is to expect to do this but not get around to it at all, or leave it so long after the event that any cryptic notes to yourself have lost their meaning by the time you read them. If you find you respond well to deadlines, consider buddying with another participant. Commit to sharing your reflections with each other at a specified date in the future, for instance 1 or 2 weeks after you return. A triad may work even better as with three in the group at least one is likely to spur the other two to share their reflections. You may decide to send yourself a postcard 3 or 6 months after the event, reminding yourself of actions that you committed to take.

Think about the conference as a whole and ask yourself the following questions:

What were the key messages? What stood out for you as significant? If you reflected on each day or part of the day, review your notes. Can you see a pattern in your reflections? Are there themes or ideas that have particular resonance for your institution or department?

This may help you to identify key themes in your field, but it may also help you to focus on key points for you individually. Perhaps there are issues that you would like to learn more about, areas that appear to be emerging about which you have limited knowledge. Make a plan for follow up activities. Share this plan with your triad and offer feedback on their plans. Are they realistic, are there alternative ways to achieve the same outcome that you could suggest?

Revisit the notes that you took on individual sessions. Are there any action points that you would like to note and follow up? Are there messages you would like to share with your colleagues or the administrators in your department or institution? If so, what would be the best way to share? It may be appropriate to write a conference blog, for example.

Would you recommend this conference to someone else? If this is an annual event this may be of practical use – should you or someone else go next time it is held? If it is a one-off event still ask yourself this question – was this a good use of time and budget, why?

At the Teaching Commons at York University we have recently started to share our impressions about conferences. These are published on our website and are intended for use by ourselves as well as others. The act of making our reflections public helps us to think about the conference, and the commitment to sharing them ensures we do engage in the reflection. This is useful whether several or only one of the team attended an event. Those who attended learn from each other's reflections, while those who did not go get a snapshot of the conference content.

Depending on your role and seniority, you may have the opportunity to apply your learning directly at your institution, for example, by trying out a new approach. If you feel you are not able to take direct action, for instance regarding a change at an institutional level, the conference experience may have provided sufficient ammunition for you to use to encourage other more senior people to consider. When reviewing your notes, look at themes within the conference but also stay tuned to links and resonances with other sources such as government announcements, your reading and listening to colleagues. This may help you to identify a new concern or initiative at an early stage.

3   Following up with Contacts

Review the business cards collected during the conference. If you took the advice offered in the previous chapter you will have written a note to yourself to help you remember why you kept this particular card. If you did not do so at the time do so now before you forget.

How might you follow up with contacts? The simplest way to follow up is to send a brief email, reminding the person that you met and possibly referencing your conversation or a connecting point from the conference. If you have a particular reason for following up make it easy for the person to respond. For instance, suggest a future action or project, or invite them to a specific event.

If the reason for the connection was less specific in intent, but you are keen to maintain contact, consider something a little more traditional such as sending a postcard or reaching out through social media. Force yourself to contact everyone whose email or business card you collected. Make a note to send another message a couple of weeks later if they do not respond the first time. Then stop. If people do not wish to respond that is fine, but perseverance can pay off.

Do not restrict your contacts to people you spoke with at the conference. It may be appropriate to send an email to a presenter or keynote speaker who make a particular impression on you. You could also consider thanking the conference organizers. If you receive a request to provide feedback about the conference do make the effort to do so, as this is invaluable for the organizers, as we discuss in Part 3.

If you wish to take the task of networking very seriously build and maintain a spreadsheet or data base with contact information, notes about meetings and discussions and possible future ventures. This may be appropriate for some contacts if not for all. When you attend another conference review the attendance list to see if any of your former contacts are attending. Seek them out and remind them of your previous conversation.

4   Building on Your Learning

Go back over the schedule – what were the key learning points from each session? It may not be the learning that the presenter intended, it may not be new, it could be reinforcement of something you had already considered.

Revisit the notes that you made. With a little hindsight you may be able to spot overarching themes or emerging concerns that were not obvious at the time. Are there gaps in your knowledge that you need to address? If so, how might you do that? Take a critical stance to the arguments and ideas you have encountered. Are there flaws in the logic? Can you implement new approaches in your practice?

Think about the content of the session but also the format. Are there approaches you could use in your own work, for instance, or behaviours you would like to avoid. Treat every session as a learning opportunity.

If there was a particularly inspirational keynote, for instance, might it be worth suggesting this person as a speaker, to those who organize your institutional conference? Research the speaker's work, there may be articles and books written by them that will help you expand your knowledge or provide critical guidance for your institution. Follow up on references the speaker made during their presentation, the work of other related speakers and writers may be of crucial importance.

   Write a conference review for your colleagues. This will be appreciated by those who were unable to attend as well as whoever paid the bill. Share the review with others who attended, either at your own institution, or further afield. Compare notes. The presentation you thought was inspirational may have contained imprecise information according to someone else, or alternatively they may have spotted some key information that you missed. Follow the advice we give to students regarding study groups reviewing a lecture.

   Put your learning into practice. This may involve engaging in further research to find out more about the idea. It may require you to convince others to try out a new approach or buy some software.

5   Sharing Knowledge with Others

There are many ways to share your learning from conferences. If you presented a session consider repeating it for the 'home crowd'. Consider this also to share your impressions from the conference. If more than one of you attended from your department or institution consider presenting together to colleagues who were unable to attend. There are numerous avenues for a written review, such as a blog, on your department website, in the institutional newsletter, for instance. Focus on the process as well as the content of the conference. Did you come across novel and effective ways to present information, were there approaches you could use either in your teaching or in future conferences that you attend or organize?

6   Planning for Future Conferences

Should you consider attending the same conference next time it runs? What would be the benefits? Are you likely to meet the same people? If so, is this a good or bad thing? If meeting people you have met previously enables you to build your professional network this could be a very good thing. If you feel you have learned all you can from them then it may not be a good use of your time in the future.

   When you were at the conference did you hear about other events that might be beneficial to you? If so find out where and when they are scheduled to occur.

   Think about ways to persuade your funder that having attended this conference you should be sponsored to attend another. Consider the most compelling arguments for your attendance.

For a more scholarly and thoughtful approach to academic conferences in general, see the blog 'Conference Inference' available at: https://conferenceinference.wordpress.com/about/.

Having attended a conference, you may be inspired to host one at your own institution. This could be for internal participants, or perhaps it could be a regional event based on an issue or issue that emerged at the conference you attended. If the thought of arranging a physical face to face meeting feels daunting, consider organizing an online discussion on a topic.

7   Conclusion

Make the most of the conference experience, as you would any learning opportunity. Reflect, make sense of the new information and consolidate your thinking. Plan your next steps. As this is likely to include presenting at future conferences, read on, as in the next section we provide advice on how to improve presentation skills and make maximum impact.

PART 2

Presenting at a Conference

∴

CHAPTER 4

Submitting a Proposal

Alice L. E. V. Cassidy

I work with tutors (one graduate student and all others are undergraduates who have gone through my courses and been hand-picked) on a core first year course in Mechanical Engineering at the University of Adelaide called Design Graphics and Communication. We proposed a workshop at a 2014 STLHE conference in Kingston, Ontario. Conceiving and writing the proposal helped us to examine our own learning and teaching (L&T) methodologies, and encouraged us to refocus content, delivery and intended outcomes. The session, which aimed to introduce participants to an active learning approach devised by tutors, students and the lecturer of the course, was well received by both Engineering and non-engineering academics.

After STLHE, we regrouped, re-planned and extended the workshop length to focus more closely on course practice and classroom delivery. We presented "Thinking Like an Engineer" to the Australasian Association of Engineering Education (AAEE) in New Zealand, in December, 2014. What a success! The tutors had 42 seasoned engineers "eating out of their hands". We were invited to facilitate at another university for first year design engineering students. In May, 2016, we went to the Australian Maritime College in Tasmania. The tutors are now in the process of analysing data collected from a reflective learning exercise with the Tasmanian students, to be included in a research paper they'll present at the 2016 AAEE conference.

Recently one of the tutors wrote to me: "I was offered a consultancy job in a systems engineering position for next year! The years of experience and

*learning through tutoring have definitely been valuable, and a great show
of how far it has developed my skills".*
DOROTHY MISSINGHAM

1   Introduction

This chapter considers the steps in submitting a proposal, with the value of
presenting, notes and tips on information-gathering, including location,
criteria and deadlines; conference themes and sub-themes; an overview of
common session formats; deciding to present alone or with others; writing
your draft proposal, including creating an outline, making the best use of
technology, looking for review information, double-checking criteria, and
seeking feedback; and submission and confirmation. Time spent on these
important details will give you the best chance of your proposal being accepted.

2   The Value of Presenting

It is a lot of work to seek out an appropriate conference, find out all you can
about it, propose a session, and if accepted, actually attend and present. Why
do it? Chapter 1 suggested some reasons for attending conferences; here I focus
on the reasons for presenting at a conference.

Richlin (2001), in describing the value of the scholarship of teaching and
learning, speaks about the cycle including making your work public through
publications and conference presentations. Bronstein and Ramaley (2002)
suggest that pre-tenure (early career) faculty prepare a paper for publication,
then submit it as a conference proposal while waiting to hear back from
reviewers. If accepted, you can gather useful feedback from participants. I think
that this approach is equally valuable to any presenter, not only those who are
pre-tenure. If you plan to do this, check first with the conference organizers for
which you plan to propose a session to confirm their policy. Some conferences
invite presenters to submit a paper based on their session to be published in a
Proceedings or other form of peer-reviewed resource or publication; see Zhang
and Jia (2013) and Drott (1995). If you plan to publish a paper based on your
session elsewhere, check the policies of the journal to which you might submit,
they may have restrictions around their definition of previously published
material, especially in the case of Conference Proceedings.

From my own experience taking part in a number of conferences over many
years, the people you meet and form professional relationships with (often
merging into friendships) are priceless. Also noted in Part 1, not only do you

learn more about the kinds of work being done at other institutions (and even your own!), but writing, research and conference sessions done collaboratively is a great addition to your professional portfolio (see Herteis & Simmons, 2010; McDonald, Kenny, Kustra, Dawson, Iqbal, Borin, & Chan, 2016). My involvement in this book was directly related to meeting editor Celia Popovic at one conference, then years later talking with her another time we met at a conference about the project. Other projects and publications have also arisen from networking face-to-face at conferences.

Chapters 2 and 3 provide tips for use during and after conferences. Focusing on ways to keep in touch with the people you meet at conferences is so valuable, as is finding ways to remind yourself of the sessions you take part in, to glean great ideas for your own future conference proposals.

3   Information Gathering

3.1   *Location*

Chapter 1 offers more details on this important aspect of information-gathering. Depending on the focus and format of your proposed session, location could be a key factor. I have co-led pre-conference all-day canoe and kayak excursions where the location was an integral part of planning, organization and attracting participants (Wright, Cassidy, & Monette, 2013; Cassidy, Wright, Strean, & Watson, 2015). I have led sessions focusing on the value of connecting course material to the real world, including going outside (e.g. Cassidy, 2015). In all cases where I have done this, session participants enjoyed the unique chance to leave the confines of the session rooms and halls, noting such reflections as:

> This place fosters a way of knowing. Unlike the (typical) conference space. It is new, yet feels like home.

> Experiential learning is essential for being a reflective practitioner.

We (Cassidy & Simmons, 2009) asked participants what aspects of conferences were most important to them. The following responses mirror the value of offering conference participants a chance to see something other than the inside of the venue:

> How are or might you go outside the 'norm'; what are you doing to make best use of the venue, where the venue is not 'just' the 'insides of the conference building?'

Ways to help visitors to the area experience it while at the conference. (Relates to the venue comment above)

I hope you consider proposing a session that takes advantage of the conference locale.

3.2   *Criteria*

Ensure that your proposal adheres to all aspects of the Call for Proposals. Some conferences limit the number of proposals that can be submitted by people as primary author, so watch for that if you are part of, or planning to submit more than one session.

It is common to be asked to describe some other aspects of your proposed session, separately from the Abstract (or perhaps by another name, the section that participants will see if your proposal is accepted). These other elements or sections might include how you will engage participants, the time breakdown of your session (how much time on each of one-way presentation, interactive, Q and A, and so on) and the equipment and other materials you will require. This is often done through a check-box system online. If you have questions that are not answered by the information presented, ask by emailing the organizers. As someone who has co-organized conferences, I can confirm that I was happy to help presenters and have been asked for some interesting props over the years (a hard hat might be the most unusual!).

A good way to ensure that you meet all criteria in terms of the actual proposal is to start your draft by including headings for each section of the proposal, including word limits for each section (if more than one) and any details of how your session will be peer-reviewed. See the section below on Writing your Draft Proposal for more details.

3.3   *Deadlines*

Make a note of all dates and deadlines related to submitting proposals, including, if advertised, when you might find out if your proposal has been accepted. That deadline should, ideally, be before any registration deadlines! Bookmark and return to the conference website regularly to see if any information has changed. A key deadline to make note of is an early-bird registration deadline. Also, some conferences offer a one-day rate, so given other factors noted above and elsewhere, this might be a good option to consider.

If the conference in question has both regular sessions and a special pre-conference day, look for earlier deadlines for the latter, if this is something you plan to propose. The deadlines to propose either style of session can vary widely depending on the conference. Smaller, local conferences often have deadlines that are closer to the actual event. Larger, national or international conferences often have deadlines that are long in advance (such as end of October for an early June conference).

4   Conference Themes and Sub-Themes

Most conferences have a unique theme each year. Themes are intended to inspire or intrigue those considering proposing sessions and/or attending as participants or sponsors. Visiting the conference website, you will find a brief description further explaining the theme. You may well be able to 'tweak' your session topic to the given theme or it could fit perfectly from the start.

Often, not only does a conference have a theme, but also several sub-themes, streams, topics or tracks (or you might find other terms) each with brief overviews. Sub-themes are intended to give you an even better idea of what the conference organizers are looking for, so you can focus your intended session further.

Sub-themes might, at times, be interpreted differently by those considering submitting. Consider the tracks at the 2016 International Society for the Scholarship of Teaching and Learning (ISSOTL) conference, focusing on 'Telling the story of teaching and learning': effective teaching, student learning, public discourse about teaching and learning, narrative of course design, learning to tell stories, student stories and international stories. A proposal might fit equally well into two or more tracks (such as 'student learning' and 'student stories'). For example, consider a proposed session whose title is 'Student story-telling leads to engaged learning'. Oher tracks might be explicit, e.g., 'Learning to tell stories' is likely intended for newcomers to learn more about the topic. If I were to propose a session for that track, I might call it 'A practical introduction to the use of story and narrative in teaching and learning'. In fact, I did lead a pre-conference at the 2006 STLHE conference called 'Integrating learning through narrative/story'. The theme that year was A World of Learning. Quite broad!

See the section below on titles. I suggest that you do not repeat a theme or sub-theme name in your title; it is a waste of your precious word count, and will or should be obvious to those considering attending your session. Think about how you will relate your proposed session to the conference theme or a subtheme, as some Calls for Proposals ask you to speak to this point. Do not repeat a theme or sub-theme name in your title; it is a waste of your precious word count, and will or should be obvious to those considering attending your session.

5   Common Session Formats

The next thing to consider is in which format you will propose your session. As you are deciding, peruse the website of your possible or chosen conference. You might find guidelines to help you. For example, the 2016 Conference of the Society for Teaching and Learning in Higher Education (STLHE) gave guidelines for posters and for Pecha Kucha http://stlhe2016sapes.ca/PosterAndPechaKuchaGuidelines.pdf.

The most common format types are listed below. You may find different terms for any of these. Depending on the format, it might be concurrent or stand-alone, and mainly one-way presentation or interactive. See Chapter 8 for more discussions about session formats, from the perspective of a conference organizer.

Concurrent sessions: Sometimes called parallel sessions, there could be 4–20 choices in any given time slot, depending on the size of the conference. This is all the more reason to find ways, through your proposal's title and description, to encourage people to choose yours should it be accepted.

Research paper: This type of presentation summarizes research work carried out by the presenter, be it new work or research in progress. Often based on a draft paper or even a book chapter, it might be the first time the participants will have had the opportunity to learn about the work. Though this format tends to be a one-way flow of information from presenter to participant, there can (and in my view, should) be the opportunity for questions.

Usually brief (15–30 minutes), research papers are often grouped with others – not necessarily similar – into a larger chaired session. Think of how to make your session stand out, be it part of a grouping or on its own. Do not plan to read it, but rather choose a few highlights of your work to share and bring those highlights into your proposal.

Discussion paper: Though sometimes based on a draft paper, this format could be about any topic you think will draw out interactive discussion and/or a focus on question and answer. Consider in your proposal what kinds of discussion points you might include and how you will keep the conversation moving. A provocative or controversial title and topic might be a good place to start.

Workshop: Sometimes called a seminar or simply a session, this format, usually 60–90 minutes, is an excellent way to involve participants through activities that engage them. There is nothing quite like the concentrated buzz of groups as they set off on an activity or discussion that has grabbed their imagination and stimulated their enthusiasm.

In your proposal, be sure to say how participants will be involved in the session. Participants will see the description; many base their decision to attend on how engaged they will be. Just as you use lesson planning for teaching, consider the timing, the materials, what you will do and, most importantly, what participants will do during your time together. It is advised to include learning objectives so that prospective participants know what they may know, or be able to do by the end of the workshop.

Pre-conference: Many conferences have one day of pre-conference (usually the day before the 'main conference' and sometimes at a different venue). Choices usually include half-day and full-day sessions. Pre-conference sessions are usually meant to be highly interactive and very hands-on. Ensure that you clearly describe what participants will do over the whole time of the session, and what they will take away from coming to your workshop.

Stand-alone sessions: Except for keynotes (the focus of Chapter 6) and occasional other special events (see further in this section as well as Chapter 7), there are few events at a conference where everyone is in one place for a period of time. The most common and regular kind of offering of this sort, for which you might propose a session, is the Poster.

Poster: Often associated with a reception, frequently taking place over 60–90 minutes, people walk around and view posters placed on mobile stands. At some conferences, I have seen the engaging practice of ringing a bell at regular intervals to encourage participants to move through each poster in turn. Usually, conferences give guidelines regarding the dimensions to make your poster, and explain how they will be attached to a display backing. The most effective posters make the best use of visuals, and limit blocks of text. Try to have an interactive component (ask participants to contribute in some way) and make sure to have a clear take-home message. Posters can be an excellent way to talk with a large number of conference delegates.

Recently, there has been an increase in variety of formats offered, including:

Roundtable, sometimes organized as a World Café (or, occasionally known as Critical Café): Often taking place in one large space, this type of session lends itself to a guided discussion, with no technical presentations. Participants are likely to appreciate the provision of a short handout or weblink follow-up. People might move around between tables, so find ways in your proposal to attract people to your table and topic and to stay there for the allotted time.

Pecha Kucha: Devised in 2003 in Tokyo http://www.pechakucha.org/, this very concise presentation has 20 slides presented in 20 seconds, for a total time of just under seven minutes. However different variations have developed in recent years, such as sometimes being followed by a form of roundtable or networking session. At the 2016 conference of the Society for Teaching and Learning in Higher Education (STLHE), the first time this long-running society has offered it, after three presentations, eight minutes were set aside for questions for any of the three presenters.

This is a very lively format: proposals for these sessions need to be described in equally 'punchy, concise language'. At the 2016 STLHE, Trent Tucker led a Pecha Kucha called *Why 'assigned seating' for exams is the best thing since sliced bread*. The description came in at 77 words.

Walk and Talk: I admit that I only saw this format at the STLHE conference in 2003 when I ran the academic programme and created it. But I hope to see it at more conferences! Peer-reviewed, it not only allowed more chance for presenters whose funding depends on being accepted to present, but it meets a common interest of conference participants to 'see something of the outside', be it a campus or another setting. If you see a chance to propose this type of session, aim for ways for participants to discuss as they walk, in pairs or small groups perhaps, then come back to the larger group for sharing back and further discussion.

Some recent and upcoming conferences offer such new formats as Case Studies, Student Papers and Work in Progress Reports (see more at http://www.ed-conference.org/call-for-papers.html); Panels, Spotlights and Mentored Projects (see more at http://issotl.com/conf/index.php/issotl16/index/pages/view/submissions).

The Educational Developers Caucus (EDC) 2017 conference organizers (see http://edc2017 guelph.com/) took the choice of session formats to what I see as 'the one to beat'. Talk about (Re) thinking Tradition (the conference theme)! Some new formats they offered include Silent presentations that are pre-recorded and submitted by those attending in person or at a distance, Book Club, Undergraduate Experience, Speed Dating, EDC Campfire, Human Library, Welcome to my Workshop, Writing in the Scholarship of Teaching and Learning and even Name Your Own Conference Format.

This variety is good to see. Perhaps we need more of it. When you attend a conference, you will most likely be asked to provide feedback (see more about this in Chapter 11). Don't hesitate to suggest new and different kinds of sessions, that you would like to attend.

6   Present Alone or with Others?

Do you wish to present alone or with others? Your decision will very much depend on your proposed topic, and to a lesser extent the session format. If you intend to present on work that was done collaboratively, at the very least you should consult with your collaborators. They may not be able or interested in attending the conference, in which case you should of course acknowledge their work in your individual presentation. In other situations, you might wish to consider proposing a session on a topic of mutual interest to yourself and others. For example, a group-led session at the 2016 STLHE conference focussed on taking part in reviews of teaching support centres. This grew from an online discussion between some of the presenters about the topic. As the conversation developed, a suggestion was made that this might work well at the conference and the idea was formed to submit a proposal. Not only did this lead to a highly interactive conference session, but the group is now working on a related publication.

Most conferences do not require all co-presenters to be in attendance. Find this out during your information-gathering. In fact, it is often impossible, depending on the number of co-authors. By including co-authors who might not be able to co-present in person, you acknowledge their important role in the work. I have been able to present through technology, recording a short video clip and/or having an activity I designed be part of sessions for which I am co-author but cannot physically attend. Consider these ways to work with others on conference proposals.

Working with others on conference proposals can be a very worthwhile venture, as I found in a recent project with my colleague Gary Poole. Cassidy and Poole (2016) asked educational developers for examples of the nature and value of external work that took them beyond institutional boundaries, including conference attendance.

Organizing the responses into four levels of impact (A. Participant reaction; B. Perceived Learning; C. Behaviour and Attitude Change; and D. Institution), conference-related examples formed a large part of the responses, with most responders extolling the many benefits of presenting with others, especially from other institutions:

– A. Extra work worth the gains; B. Practice diplomacy to meet common goal; C. Article in society newsletter and future collaborations; D. New colleagues work with us in the future
– A. Present regionally and internationally; B. Personal and intellectual development, for students and myself; C. Invited to facilitate at another institution; D. Bring visibility and prestige to the institution and the centre; enhance my career
– A. Present on subject I teach; C. Invited to lead keynote

I have had great success co-presenting with students. If you are focusing on teaching and learning, or as my colleague Dorothy Missingham points out, in Australia, the more common term of learning and teaching, it is extremely important to show, if you are a teacher, what techniques you use in class, and for your students to show how these affect their learning. Perhaps they are graduate students who help to lead parts of classes. In my experience, participants very much enjoy attending sessions that are co-led by teachers and students. I encourage you to try it, if you never have before.

From an organizational perspective, it takes more time and effort to propose a session with others than if you are working alone. Work backwards from the submission deadline to determine when to get started to draft a session led by two or more colleagues. My advice is that whatever timing you think might work, move the start date even further back. For example, I was the lead, working with five other colleagues, on a proposed session for the 2015 STLHE conference. Our approximate timing, working backwards and from the perspective of the lead:

Jan 23   Deadline to submit proposal
Jan 15   Write penultimate proposal and ask for last input by Jan 20
Nov 20   Write draft proposal and ask for input, noting who should comment on which parts, by Nov 25
Nov 15   Meet to brainstorm what we might like to propose

The extra-long lead-in time was necessary in this case, as term was ending in late November and people tend to disappear from campus and email communication over the Christmas Break. Once back in January, many people were busy with start of the new term. Our proposal (see Cassidy, Fu, Valley, Lomas, Jovel, & Riseman, 2015) was accepted.

Usual steps include:

- Meet as a group (face to face or electronically) to brainstorm ideas
- Keep the conference details (especially themes and sub-themes, and formats) in mind as you go
- Have a revolving chair for subsequent meetings to keep everything collegial
- Talk early on about author order and justification in terms of work load; make sure everyone is happy with the result or at least can accept it
- Share who takes and shares minutes, especially action items such as deadlines for each step
- Be clear in email communications about the deadlines to edit or write various parts of the proposal. As lead, stick to your deadlines to show that 'this is real'

– Use a shared online tool to co-write, from brainstorming through writing of drafts of the proposal and the final to submit
– Be very clear about who will submit the proposal by the deadline; this is usually, but not always, the primary author.

Of course if your session is accepted (fingers crossed!), see Chapter 5 for tips on preparing the session when working in a group, including suggested deadlines.

7   Writing Your Draft Proposal

7.1   *Start with an Outline of Your Session*
I find it useful to brainstorm first, starting with possible key words for a session I plan to propose. You could write key words or phrases on small sticky notes, then, if you like to work visually, move the sticky note key words around to create a mind map. Mind maps are simpler than concept maps (the latter where key words are connected by arrows with descriptive wording; see Cassidy, Griffiths, & Nakonechny, 2001). A mind map can mirror the way you are thinking about a topic, from the main idea to the ways the various 'bits and pieces' fit in. The order in which you refer your key words and ideas might emerge from your mind map. I illustrate with an example of my own, from the 2016 STLHE conference:

Key words I considered for the session I wanted to propose:

– First day of class – first 15 minutes (this turned out to relate closely to the title I chose)
– Interactive
– Dynamic
– Involve students
– Show enthusiasm
– Model use of syllabus in new way
– Model how I work with students
– Share techniques
– Link to literature
– Provide online resources

Mind map I created to organize key words into a likely order for the proposal (and the session):

```
                    First day of class – first 15 minutes
                                    |
                                    v
                       Model syllabus and interactivity


        Share techniques, mine and participants          Questions and comments
                        |              |                            |
                        v              v                            |
        Cite related literature  Enthusiasm statement  Course highlights
                                         \          /                |
                                          v        v                 v
                              Challenge students to motivate them
                                            |
                                            v
                              Conference stream:  Motivation
```

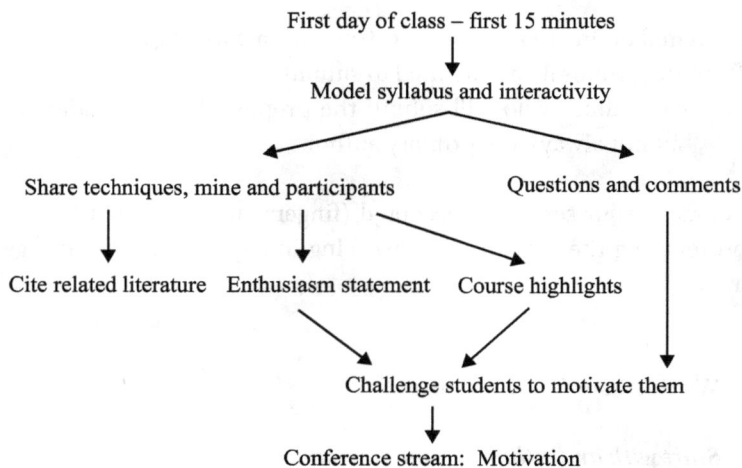

How can you start your course for best effect? Motivation is one of the most potent factors influencing student learning (Svinicki, 2004). A dynamic introduction sets the tone for the whole term. We want students to share our enthusiasm and find our courses compelling (Barkley, 2010). Course highlights, questions, expectations and challenges could figure in, as can showing students something unique about you and your approach. We will practise ways to custom-craft the first fifteen minutes of a course to motivate learners. Break away from traditional approaches! The level of motivation your students bring will be transformed, for better or worse, by what happens in class (Gross Davis, 1993). You will leave this session having participated in several techniques, including crafting (or having started) an 'enthusiasm statement' or considered other ways to share your enthusiasm for the topic. You will also have participated in other opening techniques, such as asking questions about the syllabus and the instructor, and answering questions I pose about your interest (and challenges) with the course material. You will be invited to share your own successes and consider new ideas. I will provide additional web resources for you to explore after the session is over.

7.2   Choose a Title

There are varying views on how best to do this. The key is that potential participants will have an idea of what the session is about when doing a cursory scan of the conference schedule. But do you want to 'tell all' or light their curiosity? Sometimes you can do both. I feel that a succinct catchy title can be very effective. I admit I am biased, having had success in terms of proposal acceptance and attendance at such sessions. Others believe that a title should be quite descriptive.

The above comments also relate to the use, or not, of subtitles. I feel that you should be able to get your key message across without one. Consider how specific you want to be. For example, imagine you are proposing a session about flexible learning in a 2nd year sociology course. If you include the course topic (sociology) in your title, you may attract people teaching in that discipline. Is that what you want? If so, go for it. Knowing the audience at the conference may help you decide. Is the focus on flexible learning? That would likely attract a much larger audience. What about the 2nd year or lower level aspect? Again, it depends. The more you narrow down your title, the fewer potential participants will see it being relevant to them.

Increasingly, conference organizers provide complete session descriptions online only. Participants receive a small paper booklet at the conference listing titles, presenters, times and locations only. This makes it even more important that the title attract the right audience. Some people will plan ahead and read the full description. Certainly, those who have read and taken the advice in Part 1 of this book will do so! But, not everyone has easy access to the online material. So, many people (perhaps the majority) will base their decisions on which session to attend purely by reading the titles and noting the name of the presenter.

7.3   *Make the Best Use of Technology*

It's a good idea to first create your proposal 'off line' in a word-processing or text-editing programme, so that you have everything in one place rather than entering the information directly on to the website. Once you start completing what is most often a web-based application, it is easy to copy and paste into the online system. This approach means you will have your original to know what you entered (through copy and paste). This can be particularly useful should the online system stop working, for whatever reason, before you complete the online submission.

If it is possible, go through that online system first to determine the elements or sections required and their word limits. Some conferences post this information as a PDF or in another form, making it easier to see at a glance. Make sure you are clear about which of these sections (often called the Abstract) prospective participants will read. Earlier, in Criteria, I outlined some tips for preparing your proposal by considering all of the sections needed early on.

7.4   *Look for Review Information*

Is the review process documented on the conference site? If so, read this carefully. Put yourself in the shoes of a reviewer, to ensure that you meet all criteria and address everything that reviewers will be looking for. Consider offering to be a reviewer for the conference. Not only is it a great way to contribute, but you can learn a great deal about the style of proposals submitted. This may help you for a future submission. You might want to look for review information before you start your outline, or after you have your first draft, while you are double-checking criteria. Some conferences post the review rubric or form to be used, or present it in a list, such as with the 2017 Transformative Learning Conference.

7.5   *Double-Check Criteria*
You have written your first draft proposal. Now go back to the conference website and check what you have against the criteria, reviewer information if it exists, and any other information about proposing a session. You cannot do spell checks and careful proof-reading too many times!

7.6   *Seek Feedback*
Show your title and the full description or other aspects of the proposal to a few colleagues, for a second or third set of eyes. All the better if they have taken part in the particular conference. Would they attend your session if it was accepted? What might improve it, both from content and process perspectives? Many people leave it to the last minute to write their proposal and submit by the deadline, precluding the chance for feedback. Starting early and seeking feedback is highly recommended, for a greater chance of having your proposal accepted. Use the feedback you are provided to hone your proposal. Even though you may have looked at the proposal a number of times, you may miss something obvious that another reader will notice. This gives you the chance to adjust for enhanced clarity of message.

8   Submit Your Proposal

Submit your proposal at least a few days before the deadline, to account for any last-minute technical challenges. It is not unusual for conference organizers to extend deadlines, often doing so close to the original submission date. Do not count on this by any means. If you have worked through your proposal with plenty of lead-in time, and submitted before the deadline, you will be ahead of the game should the organizers, for whatever reason, choose to extend it.

8.1   *Confirm*
Ideally, the conference online system will keep you informed, perhaps by providing status reports or access to follow the progress of your proposal. If the

conference website gave a date by when you should hear, watch for something in your email If you don't get a message, first check in your junk or spam email. If you have still not received confirmation, contact the conference organizers. A session I proposed recently 'fell through some electronic cracks'. When two other sessions I was involved in as a co-presenter had been confirmed as being accepted, I waited another day or two to hear about the one I proposed to lead on my own but still did not receive word. When I contacted the organizers, they told me that, yes, my session was accepted and did not know why I was missed in their messaging system. It was a good lesson. You ought to be notified if your session is accepted (and if so, with reviewers' feedback and any requested changes) or if it was not accepted (ditto, with reviewer feedback to help you next time.)

9   Concluding Remarks

If this is your first conference proposal, congratulations on starting on what I am sure will be a fulfilling path. And to do a good job is a lot of work. If this is your 3rd, or 30th conference proposal, congratulations for continuing on this path, and you already know it is a lot of work. You will also know that you will receive and be expected to incorporate reviewer feedback to make your session the best it can be. See Chapters 5 and 6 for details of preparing and presenting your session, should it be accepted, starting with making full use of reviewer feedback. Attention to these important details helps all of us as teachers, educational developers, conference presenters and participants.

References

Barkley, E. (2010). *Student engagement techniques: A handbook for college faculty.* San Francisco, CA: Jossey-Bass.

Bronstein, J., & Ramaley, J. A. (2002). Making the persuasive tenure case: Pitfalls and possibilities. In J. E. Cooper & D. D. Stevens (Eds.), *Tenure in the sacred grove: Issues and strategies for women and minority faculty* (pp. 31–55). Albany, NY: State University of New York Press.

Cassidy, A., Fu, G., Valley, W., Lomas, C., Jovel, E., & Riseman, A. (2015). *Flexible learning strategies in first through fourth-year courses.* Society for Teaching and Learning in Higher Education Conference, Vancouver, June.

Cassidy, A., Griffiths, T., & Nakonechny, J. (2001, September). Tapestry, Newsletter of the Centre for Teaching and Academic Growth, 4. *Concept mapping: Mirroring processes of thinking and learning (Tapestry, Volume 4: Newsletter of the Centre for Teaching and Academic Growth).*

Cassidy, A., & Poole, G. (2016). Using social network analysis to measure the impact and value of work that takes us beyond institutional boundaries. *International Journal for Academic Development, 21*(4), 323–336.

Cassidy, A. L. E. V. (2015, June). *Go outside and learn!* Paper presented at Society for Teaching and Learning in Higher Education Conference, University of British Columbia, Vancouver.

Cassidy, A. L. E. V., & Simmons, N. (2009, February). *Conference pedagogy: Change can be good.* Educational Developers Caucus Conference, Durham College, Oshawa.

Cassidy, A. L. E. V., Wright, W. A., Strean, W. B., & Watson, G. P. L. (2015). The interplay of space, place and identity: Transforming our learning experiences in an outdoor setting. *Collected Essays on Learning and Teaching, 8*, 27–34. doi.org/10.22329/celt.v8i0.4242

Davis, B. G. (1993). *Diversity and complexity in the classroom: Considerations of race, ethnicity and gender.* Retrieved from https://www.indiana.edu/~istr695/readingsfall2013/Tools%20For%20Teaching.pdf

Drott, M. C. (1995, May). Reexamining the role of conference papers in scholarly communication. *Journal of the American Society for Information Science, 46*(4), 299–305.

Herteis, E. M., & Simmons, N. (2010). *The portfolio process: Green guide no. 10.* London: Society for Teaching and Learning in Higher Education.

McDonald, J., Kenny, N., Kustra, E., Dawson, D., Iqbal, I., Borin, P., & Chan, J. (2016). *Educational development guide series: No. 1. The educational developer's portfolio.* Ottawa: Educational Developers Caucus.

Richlin, L. (2001). Scholarly teaching and the scholarship of teaching. *New Directions for Teaching and Learning, 2001*(86), 57–68.

Svinicki, M. (2004). *Learning and motivation in the postsecondary classroom.* Bolton, MA: Anker.

Wright, A., Cassidy, A., & Monette, M.-J. (2013). Paddling through time: Learning for life in the coastal zone. *Society for Teaching and Learning in Higher Education (STLHE) Newsletter, 62*, 1–2.

Zhang, Y., & Jia, X. (2013, July). Republication of conference papers in journals? *Learned Publishing, 26*(3), 189–196.

CHAPTER 5

Preparing and Presenting Your Session

Alice L. E. V. Cassidy

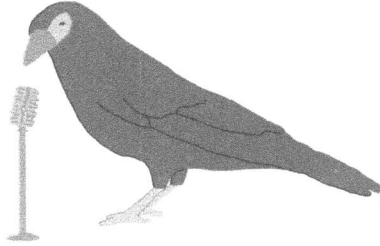

My first presentation at a higher education conference was completely improvised. I was in Montpellier, France for the Association internationale de la pédagogie univesitaire (AIPU), an international conference of experts and practitioners. For the very first presentation the speaker hadn't shown up but 30–40 participants were waiting. Rather than waste our time, I proposed to the host representative that I give a workshop based on Chickering and Gamson's (1987) Best Practices in Undergraduate Education. Luckily, a few months back, Paola Borin and Erika Kustra had presented a magnificent workshop on the subject at University of Ottawa and their experiential exercises were simple, effective and very interactive. I had no material, slides or preparation but my colleagues were willing so off we went! I adjusted some of the activities since I had no props. Everyone enjoyed the experience.
    BOB PARSON

1 Introduction

Your session has been accepted and now it is time to get ready to present it. This chapter, which builds on Chapter 4, focuses on planning, preparing and presenting your session.

I begin with guiding principles for optimal learning in conference sessions. You will read tips about planning your session, including using the abstract of your proposal as a starting point, connecting to the conference and your prospective audience, confirming the room layout, technology and supplies, and creating a planning document much like a lesson plan, to assist in your organization and guide you during the session. Planning with a group has its own special set of tips. I will describe ways of presenting, including use of flipcharts, handouts, projected presentations and use of other formats and materials. Posters have their own special section.

You have planned your session and now you are ready to present. I'll discuss ways to be ready before, and just as your session starts, including visiting your room in advance. I will focus on ways to involve your participants, including 'changing on the fly' as needed. You may occasionally find yourself leading a session you did not think you would be leading. I'll suggest ways to keep calm and stay on time, how to address the unexpected, as well as to seek feedback from participants to help you grow as a conference presenter.

Imagine it is the day and time of your session. You are ready and in the space you were assigned. People are moving from room to room to attend a lot of sessions, often with little time to spare. If a poster session, they are moving around one large space deciding at which posters they will stop and explore. What have you done to prepare, and will do in presenting to make yours an especially pleasant experience for them and one that is memorable?

Guiding principles for optimal learning in conference sessions:

- Match your session to your proposal
- Confirm details
- Decide how to present
- Make a plan
- Involve your participants
- Practice
- Check things out on site
- Stay calm and on time
- Seek feedback from participants
- Provide a follow-up
- Make them glad they came

2   Match Your Session to Your Proposal

Your proposal has been accepted, based on your abstract and/or other elements or sections asked for in the process. Great! Now is the time to 'walk the talk' and do what you said you would do. Take full advantage of the good work you have done to date. Use the Abstract (or whatever name is used to describe your session in the conference programme) of your proposal as a starting point, and be true to it; this is no time to adjust what you proposed, or start from scratch. Be aware that most of your participants will have chosen to attend your session based on the description. Be mindful about honouring this informal contract.

3   Confirm Details

Remind yourself, by looking at the conference website and any subsequent emails from the organizers, about specific details. First, check the session format, and any related information about it, such as theme or sub-theme, expectations, exact amount of time allotted and the room in which your session is booked.

If this is your first experience of the conference, re-confirm its nature or focus and your prospective or intended audience This information may be available on the. conference website. If you indicated the session was aimed at a particular group, e.g., graduate students or biology professors, be sure to keep that in mind as you plan your session.

If you can do so ahead of time, confirm the room layout, technology and supplies available. Check the conference information to establish whether you can expect your technical needs will be met. If in doubt, contact the conference organizers to ask. It is a good idea to bring a back-up for common disasters, bring your presentation both on your own laptop computer and on a USB stick.

Just because you requested it, and even if you were told it would be there, do not bank on it. If something is essential to the smooth and successful running of your session, bring it with you. You may wish to create and bring a 'must have' presentation kit. What is in it depends on your presentation style: sticky notes, index cards, coloured pens, a few folded pieces of flipchart paper, masking tape, headache medicine, reading glasses (okay, some of these items might be of a more personal nature...!).

4   Decide How to Present

There are numerous ways to make your presentation memorable. If you would like it to be interactive, consider the possible uses of such things as flipcharts and handouts or more unconventional formats and materials such as the use of props or processes (see also Table 5.1).

Is your session mainly a one-way presentation (e.g. presenting research findings) or an interactive session? If the former, a talk is not the same as a paper. Check with the organizers about the convention for this conference. In some it is expected that the presenter reads a paper. Unless this is specifically required, avoid doing this as it is invariably dull as people can read your paper for themselves. There are numerous ways to present data. For example, instead of going through each slide describing the data, show the slide then give participants a few minutes to look it over, then ask questions, or ask them how they might connect this data set to the overall idea of the topic. I have experienced this technique as a participant in conference sessions and as an attendee to an invited speaker series. I enjoy the chance to take part actively in what might otherwise be a one-way talk.

Consider providing handouts. If they are to be used by participants during the session to make notes or write reflections, be sure to bring more than you think you will need, so you do not run out. Alternatively consider using an online solution. Most conference participants bring laptops or tablets to sessions, but you may not be able to guarantee this. Bring a few paper handouts and make an outline copy available for participants to download and use in your session.

If you are presenting an approach or technique, consider modelling it in your session. For example, for a session about Problem-based Learning, you might ask for volunteers, then give them an actual case used in PBL in your field, and as they walk through (at least a sample of) what your students do, have others in the audience take notes... decide how much time to spend in order to debrief, and/or address other aspects you proposed. In a session focused on ways, as a teacher, you help your students to learn effectively, are you able to include a student as a co-presenter? Alternatively include an audio or video clip of a student explaining the approach. This approach is both more authentic and engaging for participants than the traditional lecture style presentation.

Be scholarly in your work, for instance, by connecting to the work of others in your session, by providing and acknowledging references.

An important part of deciding how to present is to consider the room layout (see Section 7 below). If you have flexibility once on site, consider the best arrangement to match your abstract and how you plan to involve participants. If you are allocated a fixed tier seated lecture hall, for example, it may not be easy to include physical activity in your session. If necessary, ask the organizers if it is possible to change location by trading rooms with another presenter. It is best, if possible, to arrange this early enough that your room makes it into the programme, thus avoiding confusion on site. See related tips in Sections 7 and 8 below.

5   Make a Plan

Consider your own preferences in terms of presentation style. Some people are very comfortable facilitating a flexible, open ended session, while others are more confident in a highly structured event. Play to your strengths. Even the most structured session may contain participant engagement. However, if you force yourself to do something that does not fit well for your style, it is likely to be less successful than an approach where you can excel. Giving a conference presentation has parallels with teaching, but it also has differences. In a conference presentation, you may have only this one opportunity to convey your message. You will wish to do so effectively. There is unlikely to be the equivalent of a follow up class to address misconceptions.

Create a planning document to guide you during the session. This is a detailed guide to the session with timings, actions and any props or resources required. This document will help you use your allotted time most effectively. There are two ways to do the timing, either use the actual time, e.g. 12.00 as the start, or use the allocated minutes, e.g. 0 to 60. This may sound trivial, but it can have an impact in the heat of the moment. If the session begins later than anticipated, the stated clock times may throw you off. It may be easier to adjust the plan in situ if you use 0 to 60. Make your choice based on what will be easiest and clearest for you to use.

Chapter 4 provided tips on writing your proposal, using keywords and a mind map. A completed proposal based on this approach was included as an example. I illustrate a plan that was used for that session, see Fig. 5.1.

A couple of notes about this example:

The timing does not start at 0 minutes. In my experience, no session has ever started exactly on time. Having a buffer helps you to adjust your timing no matter how delayed the session is in starting.

The times noted are the 'latest' time it should be. If you find yourself ahead of time, you know you have even more of a buffer, but do not start taking that for granted.

Participant activities tend to take more time that you might think. Even with experience, it is wise to build in extra time for this. A simple show of hands may not take long, but if you ask for examples people invariably talk longer than you might anticipate. Think-pair-share or group discussions can take the longest time, so make sure you allow plenty of time for this. See more details in Section 5 below.

Though the session in this example is 50 minutes, the timing ends at 46 minutes. It is far more likely that you will start to run out of time near the end, so leave yourself a buffer, as described above. If you really have finished everything you planned, you can simply ask if there are other questions, or comments.

Plans do not always reflect reality. At a session a colleague and I presented many years ago, we started, as many sessions might, by asking people to introduce themselves to one other person and say why they came. We stopped

Total timing: 50 min

3 min	Welcome! One of the streams in this year's conference is Motivating Students. Show slide: Education is not the filling of a pail. Comments?
6 min	Pre-test: Knowledge in the area of Motivation
11 min	Give a couple definitions of Motivation and relevance to T and L
13 min	Who is here?
	Show of hands: First STLHE conference? Been to a few? Been to lots?
	Teach one or more credit courses. Learner in a course. Course designer, educational developer, administrator, researcher, other?
15 min	Welcome to class slide – build a community.
16 min	Present my 'enthusiasm statement' – how I love teaching and facilitating. My hope is to give you tools you can use right away!
	Barkley quote and rainbow
	Blue birds example
18 min	Give out 'course syllabus' for today (have used symbols on them to be able to ask individuals to contribute.)
	Take a look at the course syllabus. What question do you have about the syllabus or me as your instructor/facilitator? Talk to your neighbour. Is their question similar or different? Who has a question for me?
25 min	In my syllabus, I included my teaching philosophy to show you how I approach teaching (and facilitating). How might you show students what is unique about your approach? A suggestion?
28 min	The value of sharing your enthusiasm
	My fir cone example
34 min	Some ideas: Craft (or start) an 'enthusiasm statement' – does someone have an example?
36 min	What might be some ways to share your enthusiasm for the topic? An idea?
38 min	Another success not yet mentioned you will share?
40 min	Post-test – return to the Pre-test Qs.
44 min	Thumbs poll: Improvement? Thumbs up
	Poorer? Thumbs down
	About the same? Neutral
46 min	I will provide additional web resources for you to explore after the session is over.

FIGURE 5.1   *Craft the first 15 minutes of your course to ignite student interest.*

people after a few minutes and continued with the rest of the session (which was quite interactive.) Afterwards, we mused on leading a session sometime called something like "Who is here?" and not only starting that same way, but having nothing else planned for the rest of the session and running it completely by what participants wanted to talk about. This open ended approach has obvious challenges such as how to describe the expected outcomes but can be rewarding. See Chapter 8 for more ideas of unconventional types of session.

5.1   *Planning with a Group*

In Chapter 4, I shared examples of deadlines and steps in preparing and submitting a proposal with a group. Once accepted, keep the momentum going to plan and lead the session. It should come as no surprise that working with a group has its pros and cons. Presenting with a group can show participants the truly collaborative nature of your project or study. Keeping on track and on time is an extra challenge (even if the group size is two, it has been my experience).

Be sure to give strict deadlines for responses to each part of the planning. What might happen if someone stops replying or contributing? They are already a co-author. It is up to you, but one suggestion is to leave them off the presenting roster.

Below I present timing and related tips that I have found helpful. Conferences will differ in the 'lead-in time', from when you find out your session is accepted, to when you will present it. Using what I have found to be the shortest lead-in time, I note timing in the style of 'days before session'. Of course, as soon as you, as lead author, find out the session is 'on', you will share the good news by email or in person with your collaborators. And, as described in Chapter 4 about working with a team, you may be meeting face to face or electronically. Tips are built into the timing below.

5.1.1   60 Days

Arrange to meet as soon as possible. Make sure everyone has the accepted Abstract in hand, as well as any other aspects of the proposal that were submitted.

Start by checking in. Is everyone going to be at the conference in person? If not, how might those not in attendance contribute? You will find examples in Section 3 above. Are there any questions about what we are presenting? Next, brainstorm ways to best create a lesson plan, of the sort shown in Section 4 above. As lead, you should offer to create a first draft of the lesson plan.

5.1.2   50 Days

Share the draft lesson plan with the group. You may wish to suggest who presents each part then discuss in a meeting or by email. Plan for success by considering individual personalities and styles. For example, a very dynamic speaker might start the session by welcoming participants, making sure they are in the correct room. Another member of the group who has experience leading interactively may take on an opening ice-breaker or other way to involve all participants. If a member of the group has a reputation for going well past their allotted time, speaking frankly about this may or may not help. It might be best to suggest that person's part be near the end of the session, or that they take on another important task that does not involve speaking!

Who will create the projected slides? The lead author may be the one to keep a master copy of the slides, with others sending in those they create. What about handouts or other material needed? Organizing each of the important aspects of the session can take some time. Agree to come to the next meeting with these jobs completed. Send reminders to ensure this is done.

5.1.3   30 Days

Re-confirm the various tasks to prepare for, and during the session. Will someone other than the presenter who is speaking forward the slides? Are there other jobs besides presenting? In my experience, tasks taken on by group members have included such things as adding contributions to a wiki during the session, handing out material at various points in the session, collecting flipcharts or other items created by participants and/or keeping discussion groups on task.

How will all of you stay on time? Having an electronic timer where all the presenters can see it might help. Or, one person's job could be to cue time left, with hand signals (if each speaker pays attention to those!)

5.1.4   20 Days

Do a dry run, ideally with some colleagues taking on the roles of participants. Even if you don't have that, walking through the lesson plan, treating it as seriously as when you actually do it, can illuminate timing or other issues to be adjusted.

5.1.5   As Needed

Confirm and reconfirm all aspects of the session. Who is bringing the slides (on a USB or?) Who is bringing a laptop for presenting? Is each person bringing the hard-copy materials they are using for 'their part' or is one person (the lead perhaps) bringing everything?

5.1.6   Day of Session

Agree on time and place to meet. This could be to make sure you are all in the assigned room (or out in the hall if another session is taking place) well before your session starts. It could be to alleviate any last-minute jitters, to do a group cheer, or to check in on who is doing what and when. There may even be last-minute adjustments as a result of the room, the make-up of the group, or something else.

Two final tips:

1 This guide is based on having 60 days from the time you learn your session is accepted, to the day you co-present. You may well have more time. If this is the case, continue to start early and keep tight deadlines, as it is easy to think you have all the time in the world and there is no need to meet or plan 'until closer to the conference'. Slippery slope, my friends. Getting it all ready as early as possible is always best. Good wishes for a great group-led conference session.

2 If your group-led session is a poster, same rules apply. As described in Chapter 4 and built upon below, most poster sessions at conferences have set times or 'receptions' when one or more authors, for group-led posters, are to be 'at their poster' So in your planning meetings, add in the detail of who will 'attend' the poster, when, to welcome people, answer questions, encourage participation, and give out handout versions, if your poster has those elements. You may wish to have an informal schedule so that each of you can send the other off to get refreshments, see other posters, and/or network.

5.2 *Posters*

In Chapter 4, I note how some conferences give guidelines for posters and cite one conference's website. There are many guidelines online. Bracher, Cantrell, and Wilkie (1998) and Akister (2000) incorporate posters as experiential learning activities and course assignments, their assessment techniques provide some tips for newcomers to posters for conferences. See Figure 5.2 in Section 9 for a simple feedback form designed for posters.

The conference organizers may provide details regarding poster dimensions and means of display. Contact the organizers if you cannot find this as it will impact on the poster design.

Dimensions: Often, mobile poster stands are provided with numbers or names to indicate the location of each poster. These stands are usually of uniform dimensions, but you do not want your poster to 'hang over' or not be able to be attached properly. You might be sharing a poster stand with another presenter and the space allotted to each will hence be limited. Check with the organizers.

Backing/attachment information: If the backing is corkboard-like, then push pins will be the most logical way to attach posters. Another common way to affix posters is using a kind of two-way tape or something involving a hook and fastener type of system. Find out whether these items are supplied or if you need to bring them.

Guidance for sessions applies to an extent to posters. Be sure to provide what you promised in the abstract and think about the key or 'take home' message that you aim to provide.

Presentation software can be used to create a poster in the form of a single slide. Ask your colleagues who have made posters in this way for a template they could share. Check that the settings reflect those of the required dimensions for the current conference. I have borrowed templates from colleagues and inserted my own information. Some institutions have templates that include their logo, colours or other identifying information. Look into this early on. Leave plenty of time to complete and proofread your poster, and to meet deadlines for printing. You might want to do a web search for images (try 'academic posters') for ideas on how to create an appealing poster.

Smith, Myers and Myers-Smith (2007) provide tips for effective posters, some that also apply for projected presentations:

- Ample blank space
- Plain background that contrasts well with font colour
- Font that is a minimum of 28 point
- Good mix of print and images
- Graphs instead of tables (this may depend on your topic and format)

Smith et al. (2007) suggest clearly indicating the best 'flow' of the poster (what to read or look at in what order). Proof-read your poster several times before sending it for printing. Check spelling and grammar. Review font size, colour and layout. This is where having one or two colleagues taking a look at your draft poster can really help. You are likely too close to the topic and details to see any failings or confusing points. Project your poster as large as you can when you and colleagues do your proofreading. They may find something you were 'blind to'. Having fresh eyes will help you adjust for best effect at the conference.

If you take a paper poster, decide whether to have it laminated. Paper posters need to be rolled and transported in a special protective tube. Laminating your paper poster can provide protection in transport, and is a good choice if you plan to display it in your office or a hallway once the conference is over, or reuse it at another event. If you know you will show the poster only once, lamination adds one more material that makes recycling difficult or impossible and may be an unnecessary expense. In some cases, it may be possible to re-use a poster at a different conference. Bear this in mind when deciding whether or not to include the conference title or logo on the poster. If you are likely to re-use the poster consider printing it on cloth. This has the added advantage that it can be gently folded and stored in conventional luggage.

Seek out examples of both cloth and paper, laminated or not, to help you decide what is right for you. Also, as noted above, details of backing board and how to attach your poster are worthy of consideration in terms of what format you have your poster printed. I have seen both paper and cloth posters on the same backing boards at many conferences.

If the poster session includes a presentation or conversation with participants, plan what you would like to say. It may be appropriate to bring a handout and to come equipped with business cards or promotional material such as post cards containing links to your work and contact details.

6   Involve Your Participants

I began by suggesting that you match the abstract to your session. An important part of this process is to review the activities you described in the abstract and be sure to include them in your session plan.

Table 5.1 shows some common techniques aimed at interaction, indicating the approximate amount of time each can take. I have based these on my experience designing and leading a large number of workshops, seminars and conference sessions. This is just a guide. Below the table are further details of some of the techniques.

Brainstorm: Be clear what the topic is, and first explain that the idea is to get down as many ideas in a short period of time as possible. There is no judgment, discussion or paraphrasing (if you are noting them down as they are shared.) You might tell participants that in brainstorming, often the most creative ideas come near the end. Explore more about brainstorming at https://en.wikipedia.org/wiki/Brainstorming If you use this technique be clear how this will be used. For example, if you are generating ideas to assist you in future research make this clear to the participants beforehand.

Value line: Ask individuals to take a stance on an issue (or teaching technique), then have them stand on an imaginary line on the floor. Tell people in advance that it can be their true view or a persona they are taking on (this can make it feel less risky.) The middle is neutral; one end is agree completely, disagree completely. Now ask them to talk to people nearby about why they chose where they are standing. Ask for examples from each of three areas. Now see if anyone moves as a result. An example of an issue I have used is: "research about student learning does not promote good teaching", and a teaching technique I have used is: "I am very likely to use song as a form of narrative in my class". Explore more about value lines at https://cassidyinview.wordpress.com/in-class-activities/group-work/cbam-concerns-based-adoption-model-and-value-line/

TABLE 5.1   *Conference session techniques and timing*

Activity	Approximate time it will take (in minutes)	Other notes
Show of hands: Ask questions that can be answered in a binary fashion (yes or no), or ask for responses to a series of possible answers. May use clickers or apps that use cell phones for a technological alternative with more options.	<1 per question	Ask one Q at a time, ensuring it is clear who should put up their hand.
Brainstorm: These are unfiltered without judgement. The list generated is used in some way either in the session or some follow up activity. See below for more information.	1–5	Ask people to offer ideas in response to a stimulus. Write suggestions on flipchart or type into the presentation as they share. There are apps as mentioned above, that can be used to do this more efficiently than writing by hand.
Pre-test/post-test: Before the presentation assess the mood or attitudes or knowledge of the participants. Ask the same question after the session to see if the presentation has impacted on the answers	1–2	Project 1–4 pre-test Qs and ask participants to note down for themselves. For post-test, project same Qs, give same amount of time to complete, but now ask for private thumb vote', how many improved, stayed the same, or declined?
Ask participants: to share an example or answer a question you pose to them.	2 per contribution	Ask for it to be brief (1–2 sentences), or if appropriate, a phrase or a few words only.

Activity	Approximate time it will take (in minutes)	Other notes
Think-pair-share (TPS): Ask people to think about something on their own, then share their idea with the person next to them. You might then do Think-pair-square-share (TPSS), where then two pairs next form a quartet. Finally ask some to share a selection of ideas with the whole group.	4–6 for their work, plus 2 per example you ask to be shared	Working with just one other person can be in any setting. For tiered seating, TPS can be followed by TPSS by having pairs turn to a pair in another row.
Group work (4–7 per group): Set an activity or task for the group to complete in a given time.	7–15 for their work, plus 2–5 for each group to share	Have clear instructions on a slide or flipchart. Give a warning as to time left. Give clear guidelines/ timelines on how to report back.
Complete a worksheet, perhaps with a reflection or an action once participant leaves	5 minimum	Depends on how long it is, and what you'll do with it next
Value line – see below for a description	10–15	Consider if you have room to do this, and how many 'parts' to this activity you will do.

Whichever technique(s) you use, have a plan on how to keep on time, even if things get 'out of hand'. For example, imagine that you ask for an example or two (e.g. on your session topic of giving students responsibility for their own learning). You have set aside 5 minutes for this activity. Even though many hands go up, you say you will take two examples. The first person you invite begins but it is clear they will take the whole 5 minutes to share their example. What might you have done in advance to prevent this? One technique is to ask for two sentences maximum per person. Another is to ask for one example, then if you find you have time left, ask for one more from another person. If you wish to ensure that everyone has the opportunity to engage start with a think-pair-share (or think-pair-square-share). What if you now need to think 'on the fly' to move on once this person is underway? At the first possible pause, say "Thank you, can we hear one more, brief example (that is, if you still have time). If they do not pause (I have experienced this), cut them off in a polite way "We have to move on...". It is not a fun thing to do, but the other participants will thank you.

7   Practice

Practice your session, using the same materials (projections, props, etc.) that you plan to use in the session. Going over it out loud can help iron out any wrinkles, and help you see what you might want to work on more or adjust. It takes longer to 'speak' your session than it does to simply look at your slides and 'think' it through. As you practice the session, be sure to time yourself accurately.

As I am advocating that you involve your participants no matter what kind of session you are leading, you may need to 'improvise' for the timing when running through it on your own. If practicing with a colleague, invite them to take part in the active components for a more realistic trial run. If possible, present to colleagues, friends or family. Seek their views on what was clear and what needs further work.

Although you may feel self-conscious practicing in front of a colleague, it is well worth the potential embarrassment. When I did this with one of my earliest presentations I discovered I had made a huge assumption. The person who listened to me was a colleague but had no idea what I was talking about. I realized that I needed to explain more background than I had intended. If I had not practiced with the colleague I would not have discovered my error until the day of the presentation, which would clearly have been too late.

If you are nervous about speaking in front of a group, try this approach. Start by writing a word by word script for your presentation. Write it out slide by slide. Start by reading the script verbatim. Do this several times until you are completely comfortable with the content. Now jot down the key issues for each slide. There are several ways to do this. Some people prefer to use blank post cards (if so be sure to number them in case you drop them and lose the order) others prefer to keep the notes on their phone or use some other means. Ditch the script. Now use the notes to prompt you through each slide. You will still use the script from memory but you will sound more natural and confident than if you read it word for word.

8   Check Things Out on Site

Once you are at the conference, even if it is a day or two before your session, confirm the room information in the conference programme (you can often do this via the conference website before you arrive).

Visit the room your presentation will be in (you may wish to attend a session there before yours) and make sure audio-visual or other technology you plan to use is working, check what lighting is adjustable and if so, how the switches work. Consider how and if you will adjust the lighting at various points in your session.

During your pre-visit, or even earlier online if possible (some institutions and other conference venues have photographs and views of rooms online), look at the layout of tables, chairs, desks or other furniture. Ask yourself if it is configured in a way that works for how you plan to present. Think about the content and process of your session – will the room allow for your planned activities, such as group work or value lines? If not, can you change it just before your own session (a tip is to involve participants as they come into the room; I asked students in credit courses to do this and it works well.) If the furniture is fixed and cannot be changed, think about how to adjust your session to work best in the space you have been assigned.

Amongst many other useful tips about presentations and speeches, such as one idea per slide, use of visuals, dos and don'ts of public speaking, body language, facial expressions, gestures and ways to improve your confidence, Bender (1997) also includes suggested room layouts. In rooms where furniture can be re-arranged, suggestions include for mainly presentation-based sessions: classroom (with chairs facing front in rows) or amphitheatre (chairs curved in semicircles facing front); for sessions where it is important for everyone to see each other (tables and chairs in a U-shape).

For many of my conference sessions, I have arranged tables and chairs in 'café' groupings, where 4–6 people sit at each of several tables. This orientation is very conducive to highly interactive activities. Depending on what you have people doing, they can stay there the whole session, or move around, such as for a World Café style of activity. I have described this activity, suitable for a roundtable conference session https://cassidyinview.wordpress.com/in-class-activities/group-work/world-cafe/modified-world-cafe-format-at-a-conference/

A web search for 'room layout for seminars' shows images of a variety of layouts, including those described above.

9   Stay Calm and on Time

Your session is about to start. You are going to do well. However, no matter how much you planned and practiced, any number of unpredictable things can happen. Stay calm, do what you can to deal with whatever might occur, adjust as you go (be prepared to change 'on the fly'), be ready to move on if needed, and enjoy the experience. Your demeanor will rub off on your participants.

In my experience, a common way that presenters get 'waylaid' is when things go wrong technically. The video you planned to show does not work as you hoped, the sound is not loud enough, you wanted to hotlink to a website but the internet is down, or any number of other mis-steps. If there is a technical assistant in the room, they may be able to solve things quickly. More often, this is not the case. As a participant, it is very frustrating to watch and wait. My advice is to do what your participants wish you might do: move on. Do not dwell on what went wrong, try not to be negative about it (or apologize more than once), just keep moving forward. Your participants will thank you.

Remember to stay calm. The more practiced you are the calmer you will feel. The 'confidence loop' will come into play whereby if you sound confident to yourself, you will feel more confident, which will make you sound more confident, and so on. To increase your sense of confidence, lower the tone of your voice, speak slowly, remember to breathe and relax your shoulders.

Here are a couple of examples of things that happened to me, and how I dealt with them:

Stuff happens: While a member of the executive for the group hosting a conference, I was leading an activity, when all of a sudden, one contact lens moved to another part of my eye, and I could no longer see clearly. I explained to the packed room what had just happened, asked a fellow executive member to step in, and I headed off to sort things out. What if you are alone? Tell the participants what has happened, give them a task (e.g., chat in pairs to formulate questions they now have about the topic, or something else), then do what you need to do to return as session leader.

Be creative: While taking part in a conference, the power went out unexpectedly half-way through the day. The upcoming presenter, who was planning to use projected slides, instead explained a graph that we could not see by outlining the axes, data points and trends using his hands to point to the wall. He kept calm and positive, used humour, and adjusted on the fly. The result was one of the best explained data sets I have (not) seen in a while!

Time flies (or is just cut short): Whatever time slot you have been given is a fixed entity. It will not change. If you start 5 minutes later than planned, even through no fault of your own, you need to finish 5 minutes earlier than intended. Even when you have all the time you expect, it has been my experience both as a presenter and a participant, that one runs short of time closer to the end of the session. My tip is to not spend an overly long time on the introduction, and to make sure to leave as much of a time buffer at the end as possible. Practice your opening sentences repeatedly and memorize them so that you do not start with a long digression. Refer to the sections above on Planning and Practice for the best chance of preventing this unfortunate but common timing phenomenon.

It is particularly important to remember this if you are one of several presenting in a joint panel or session. I have been last to present in a group of four, and because of the enthusiasm of the previous speakers, found myself with less than half the allotted time to make my presentation.

I have co-presented with colleagues, where, even though we had prepared and agreed to a timing document of who would do what, when and for how long, lo and behold, the second person 'up' went way, way overtime. It was hard to get his attention to tell him to stop. That's conference life. The lesson I took from that experience was not to work with that particular person in the future.

At a recent conference at which I was co-presenting with two colleagues, as people came into the room, our first slide was visible (the title of our session). It turned out that the room was double-booked, and some people confusedly asked if this was the other session they thought it was. We lost a bit of time sorting people out. My advice is to double-check in the programme not only that your session and room match what you thought, but that there is not another session booked in that same room at that same time. I never thought this could happen, but happen it did!

Another way to change on the fly might be presenting when you did not think you would. I began this chapter with an anecdote about a conference participant who, along with many others, discovered that the session they planned to attend did not have a presenter present. Bob Parson offered to lead an impromptu session on a related topic. In my case, when a roomful of prospective participants found no presenter, I offered to facilitate a discussion, first asking each person to introduce their self and say what drew them to this session. Do not discount this unexpected way to contribute and make the best of an otherwise missed session.

10   Seek Feedback from Participants

Consider ways to seek feedback from participants to help you to hone your conference practice. The most common way to do this is to ask participants to respond to a few questions. There are a few ways to do this based on your preference. You may choose to hand out a paper, asking participants to complete it before they leave your session. Or you may choose to give participants a web link and ask them to respond electronically.

Figures 5.2 and 5.3 include 3-question feedback forms, two per page, that can be copied and cut in half, one for posters and one for sessions (or you may choose to mix and match the style of questions). There is a template to complete at the top, not only to remind you of the session (whether you choose hard copy or electronic), but if done in hard copy, those who complete it later can still return it to you.

Poster Title. Names of presenter(s). Conference and year. Your email or mailing address.

1   I found the following part of your poster to draw me in:
    because...
2   I suggest the following change to make your poster more effective next time:
    because...
3   I would also like to say:

FIGURE 5.2   *Simple poster feedback form. You will find an electronic template, formatted two per page with space for responses, that you can adapt for your own session, at https://cassidyinview.wordpress.com/by-topic/conference-pedagogy-and-planning/ feedback-forms/simple-poster-feedback-form/*

Session Title. Names of presenter(s). Conference and year. Your email or mailing address.

1   The best part of today's session for me was:
2   One suggestion for improvement in your next session is:
3   I also want to say/observe/suggest:

See Chapter 11 for a discussion about evaluating conferences as an organizer.

FIGURE 5.3   *Simple session feedback form. You will find an electronic template, formatted two per page with space for responses, that you can adapt for your own session, at https://cassidyinview.wordpress.com/by-topic/conference-pedagogy-and-planning/ feedback-forms/simple-feedback-form-2/*

11   **Provide a Follow-up**

Depending on the type of session, you may wish to create a summary of your work available to hand out to people or to have linked on a website. If the session is based on a published paper, have your paper available to view. Depending on copyright rules for the journal, you might want to have a few copies for people to take with them, and/or available electronically. If it is a draft that you seek input on, put DRAFT in large grey letters diagonally across each page.

Consider creating a resource list or another kind of follow-up document, such as a summary of contributions, to your session. If it is something you prepared ahead of time and have in hard-copy, if it turns out that there are not enough copies, ask people to email you to request a copy. I usually provide my email address on a slide near the end of my projected slides, on a flipchart, or on something I handed out during the session. I then ask interested participants to email me. Two benefits of this: firstly, the onus is on them to contact you if they want what you have offered, and secondly, you are sure to have their correct email address (this is also less work than re-typing a sheet on which participants have printed their email addresses.)

Take business cards with your contact information (or make informal ones), so that when asked, you can give these out, at your session or during a break (I keep them in a handy place, like in my conference name tag). I find that after my session, people will come up to me to chat, ask questions or request that we stay in touch. See Chapter 2 for further advice around networking.

12   **Make Them Glad They Came**

People chose your session out of many possible alternatives. Be sure to thank participants in your closing. If you did what you said you would do, involved participants, heard their voices, and gave them a take-home message and perhaps a resource on which to follow-up, you can rest assured that they will be glad they came.

References

Akister, J. (2000). Poster presentations in social work education assessment: A case study. *Innovations in Education and Training International, 37*(3), 229–233.

Bender, P. U. (1997). *The secrets of power presentations*. Retrieved from http://www.peterursbender.com/powpres.html

Bracher, L., Cantrell, J., & Wilkie, K. (1998). The process of poster presentation: A valuable learning experience. *Medical Teacher, 20*(6), 552–557.

Chikering, A. W., & Gamson, Z. F. (1987, March). Seven principles for good practice in undergraduate education. *AAHE Bulletin*, 3–7. Retrieved from http://files.eric.ed.gov/fulltext/ED282491.pdf

Smith, J., Myers, J., & Myers-Smith, I. (2007, April). Tips for effective communication in ecology. *Bulletin of the Ecological Society of Ameri*ca, *88*(2), 205–215.

CHAPTER 6

Learning in Public: Providing a Keynote

Mary Wilson

Are you nervous? Good. You should be. Anxiety means that you are taking the enterprise seriously and your adrenalin is flowing. Without adrenalin you will be a boring speaker.
LINDA KERBER (2008)

There are few moments more professionally gratifying than when a message arrives in your inbox, or your phone rings, and you find that you have received an invitation to serve as a keynote speaker at a conference. It is thrilling to know that people respect your work and your powers of oratory enough to trust you at the podium of an important gathering of your professional community. It is flattering to learn that your colleagues are keen to hear your thinking on matters of shared interest, and it can be professionally invigorating to command the attention of a room and engage trusted peers in a focused and immediate consideration of your theories and observations about the critical questions of your discipline or profession. It can also be terrifying. It can also lead to a self-inflicted, confidence-shattering, and very public exposure to the previously undiscovered limits of your own abilities. It is not an enterprise to enter into lightly, but rather one that deserves careful forethought, planning, execution and review.

Serving as a keynote speaker at a conference brings with it unique responsibilities and unique opportunities, as well as unique professional and personal risks. This chapter will examine the burdens and privileges of composing and providing a keynote address and is intended to help you to

© KONINKLIJKE BRILL NV, LEIDEN, 2018 | DOI 10.1163/9789004373013_006

prepare yourself, thoughtfully and thoroughly, for success in this role or alternatively to recognize well in advance that it is best for you to decline such offers with grace and confidence.

1   An Invitation to Speak

In responding to the initial request, it is important to consider the proposal as objectively and dispassionately as possible. This requires you to be self-aware and self-critical about your own capabilities. Matters for consideration include your suitability and capacity to deliver a featured talk, your interest and knowledge of the conference theme or the prospective subject matter for the talk, your availability to prepare and deliver the speech, and your judgement of the plans for the conference and the work of the organizing committee.

The question of whether or not one is equipped in all capacities to take on the responsibilities associated with providing a keynote might best begin with an understanding that giving a keynote is likely to be intellectually, emotionally, and physically demanding. Those who commit to the duties of a keynote are effectively "forcing themselves to buckle down and produce research and/or writing lest they be seen to be breaking their promises, disappointing colleagues, and violating professional norms" (Gross & Fleming, 2011). Agreeing to provide a keynote address means that you will red-circle a date on your calendar for which, inescapably, a polished work must be fully born. There is no getting around the deadline for a keynote address. There will be no extensions and no excuses for late or incomplete work. If you commit, you must be assured, without equivocation, of your own ability to arrive fully prepared and with proverbial bells on to provide the promised address on the fixed date.

This can mean long hours of preparation expended in addition to the myriad other routine responsibilities one holds, so as rewarding as it can be, it can also be physically taxing to commit to the work of serving as a keynote. Busy, accomplished individuals are notoriously bad at saying "no". It is as though that word has been excised from the vocabulary of those who work so passionately and frenetically at their professional pursuits that it appears they believe that they are about to run out of runway at any moment. We all owe a debt of gratitude to these high-performing and prolific members of our community as they do keep our thinking and our activities moving ahead through their publications and projects, but if you count yourself among them, know that you too may have limits specific to keynote addresses that are imposed by the simple constraints of time. It is wise to respect and fully consider these limitations. If you are not entirely sure that you will be able to give the preparation of a keynote address all of the time it deserves and requires, then it may be best to decline the offer to speak. However, if you have great swaths of time that you can devote to preparing and polishing your talk and you feel confident in your ability to address an audience, then there are few more exciting projects to work on than a keynote address.

In contemplating an offer to provide a keynote address, do not feel compelled to answer on the spot. A well-organized conference committee will approach prospective keynote speakers far in advance, so you should have more than enough time to think and respond. If no such luxury of time is being made available, that might be a sign of the conference committee's ability to plan and execute a great conference and may introduce a need for caution and further investigation into the maturity of their plans to inform your consideration of the offer to speak.

It is perfectly appropriate to thank the conference organizers for the invitation and ask them how long you will have to consider the offer. It is wise to review plans for the conference, compose questions, and arrange for a follow-up conversation. Allow yourself the opportunity to think, with cold analysis, of the list of duties, responsibilities, and commitments that have already been set and the likelihood of being able to wedge in the demanding work of preparing a keynote with all of the inflexibility and risk associated with that particular form of academic work.

Remember that the preparation of a keynote address demands more than the preparation of a paper. It requires one to compose one's thoughts for the purposes of listening rather than reading. It necessitates memorization and rehearsal. It may also require the creation of audio-visual displays or the use of eLearning technologies or physical props suited to a large audience. Dashing off a good paper for a journal prior to receiving the benefit of feedback from editors and rounds of revisions is not the same thing as the typically solitary orchestration of a keynote. Preparing a keynote is a more isolated pursuit with less opportunity to benefit from the feedback of peers, and it can take more time. Therefore, it is important to be confident that one's workload and commitments will accommodate the need for more intense and varied effort on a fixed timeline. Factoring in the time of others is important as well if arrangements are to be made in advance for seeking feedback from trusted colleagues willing to read through or listen to your talk for the purpose of providing helpful advice. Think also of matters of work-life balance and your health and well-being. Preparing a keynote is demanding, focused work and there will be greater joy in it if there is sufficient time to approach the work with care and sufficient reserves of energy to feed on, rather than be swamped by, the stresses imposed by its performative aspects.

Aside from sober analysis of one's ability to accommodate the inflexible timeline for preparing a keynote address, it is advisable to consider that a keynote address requires a heightened degree of performance and calls upon an individual to be clear, compelling, engaging and accessible for an audience. For the keynote speaker, it is not enough to be scholarly, innovative, and insightful in one's writing. One must also be able to pull off a masterful public performance – to be compelling, but not strident; amusing, but never inappropriate; and warm, but never undignified, all in good measure. One must not drone on in a hushed monotone or rush through in loud, squeaking bursts; but rather, have the capacity to speak lyrically and move comfortably about the space as good stage actors do.

If oratory is not a particular strength, then it is possible to improve one's skills quite dramatically through focused and guided effort given adequate time to practice. Should time to improve be scant or training fail to render sufficient improvement, there is no shame in not being capable of great oratory, except of course, if one persists in pursuing public speaking opportunities and takes the stage only to suffer the public awkwardness of laboring through the performance of ideas that one might otherwise express beautifully in a written work to the benefit of one's career and edification of one's colleagues. Public speaking is not for everyone and it need not be. There is no reason to feel compelled to accept an invitation to provide a speech if public speaking is not an area in which one excels naturally or through training.

It requires a certain degree of bravery to take the stage, grip the podium, and systematically unpack one's mind in front of a captive and typically large audience of one's peers. Blumen and Bar-Gal (2006) differentiate plenary sessions from other conference sessions, characterizing keynote assemblies as "the communities' salon" and observing that "at plenary sessions, all the members of the professional community assemble, and key issues of special interest for it as well as for the general public are discussed". If the prospect of finding oneself in that situation generates more panic than excitement, it is good to know in advance where one's limits lie and then, should an invitation arrive, to have the measure of your fundamental ability to undertake such a commitment in advance. Many a respected career has taken root only in excellent written work rather than through any necessary addition of featured talks.

There are personal and professional risks in agreeing to serve as a keynote. If the keynote does not manage to prepare the address well in advance, fails to get things right, neglects to address the critical interests of the audience and themes of the conference, or somehow hits a particularly discordant note and stirs controversy, the consequences for the keynote as well as the conference organizers can be lasting. As Stanley (1995) has noted, for keynote speakers in higher education, academic identities and reputations are at stake and so it is vital to consider one's preparedness to take on the risks of serving as a keynote before agreeing to accept an offer from the conference organizers. Part of weighing those risks is coming to a full appreciation that you would be effectively agreeing to lay bare your skills, knowledge, beliefs, and values to an audience of your peers for their assessment and response. Even in the gentlest of communities, this judgement can feel weighty for a keynote speaker, so a thick skin and an earnest desire to have your work improved through interchange, can be valuable assets in those considering an invitation to speak.

When considering an offer to serve as a keynote, other matters worthy of consideration include:

- Do you feel capable of managing the performance of a keynote address in front of a large audience of your peers?
- Reflecting upon the theme of the conference, do you feel well-versed in the associated theories and practices and well-equipped to provide current insights on the theme to the audience?
- When is the conference scheduled? Is your calendar free during the conference?
- Given already committed duties and responsibilities, would you have sufficient time and opportunity to prepare well for performance on the appointed date?
- Where is the conference located and will it be possible to organize travel, accommodations, and travel documents in advance?

2 Negotiating Your Agreement

Once you have decided to accept an offer to serve as a plenary speaker, finalizing arrangements for your talk with the conference organizers should be a relatively straight-forward and painless activity, but it is certainly an important step in your planning and preparation, and one not to be overlooked. Rather than allowing informal communications and collegial handshakes to finalize plans, it is important to discuss terms and requirements formally, and produce clear documentation of the agreement between the parties. Discussing the details of the engagement in a structured way with the intent of producing an agreement to be signed can give both you and the conference organizers the peace of mind that comes from laying out the details of roles and responsibilities and expectations and help to mitigate problems resulting from miscommunications.

Matters for discussion typically include:

1 Expenses and Remuneration
   - When will you be expected to arrive and depart?
   - Will you be reimbursed for travel and accommodation expenses, or will they make arrangements on your behalf in advance?
   - If you will be reimbursed later, what are the rules regarding eligible expenses? Is there a per-diem rate? Are there travel and/or accommodation restrictions?
   - Do you have any personal requirements for travel, accommodation or food? How can these requirements be accommodated?
   - Will you be expected to register and pay for the conference and take out a membership for the society or association if you do not have a current membership?
   - What is your typical fee for a keynote address? Is that negotiable? Do the conference organizers have a budgeted amount set aside for the keynote speaker(s) that they would like you to consider?
   - Assuming you will be remunerated, will they require you to invoice them? Will they require you to have a registered business with appropriate insurance and tax status?
   - If you wish to donate your fee, will they arrange for the donation in your name and provide you with a tax receipt?
2 Publicity and Promotion
   - What arrangements will be made to promote the conference and your role as a keynote speaker?
   - Will you be required to provide a professional photograph?
   - Will they need you to provide a customized bio for the event?
   - Would they like to request a quote from you to use in promotional materials and sites?
   - Will you be providing a title for your talk or do they have a title in mind?
   - Do you have the right to approve promotional materials that go out in print form or through social media?
   - Do they require advance notice and retain the right to approve any marketing or promotion of your keynote address that you might wish to produce and share?
3 Copyright and Intellectual Property
   - Is it clear that you will retain free, unfettered, and perpetual intellectual property rights over your speech performance, any written form of your work, and any recorded audio-visuals of your performance?

- Are you subject to the copyright and intellectual property laws of the jurisdiction in which the conference event is scheduled to take place? If so, do you fully understand the implications of the laws in effect?
- Will the speaking agreement include clear statements regarding intellectual property rights that both parties will agree to observe?
- What methods can you employ to provide information regarding sources cited during your talk?

4 Delivery Requirements
- Where will the speech take place and is the space appropriate, accessible and suitably equipped for your purposes? If not, what improvements can be made?
- Will there be a podium?
- Is there a stage?
- Will there be a chair?
- Will they provide water?
- Will you be expected to provide all necessary technologies, or will they provide items including, but not limited to:
  - a computer that meets your needs, for example, has the appropriate operating system (windows or iOS), device and port configuration, graphics driver, high-speed internet connection
  - the appropriate number and location of high-definition data projector(s) or monitor(s)
  - high quality wireless and/or wired microphone (lapel/podium) and speaker system with audio controls
  - a remote clicker
- Will there be a scheduled opportunity for you to test the technologies in the room?
- What are the lighting and sound arrangements in the room?
- What are the temperature controls and how is that monitored?
- Who will be responsible for ensuring accessibility needs are met?
- Will you be required to attend any conference associated events such as receptions, dinners, press conferences, Q&A sessions or, if you have a recent publication, book signings? If so, what are the detailed arrangements and expectations for those events?
- Will your talk be recorded for sound and/or video? Are you comfortable authorizing recording? If so, what are your requirements and their responsibilities? Where will the microphones and cameras be located and will it restrict your movements on stage?
- Will you be expected to provide a print version of your talk? If so, to whom in what form and when will it be due?

3   Learning in Public

Once you have confidently determined that you are eager, able and available
to provide the keynote address and the agreement has been struck, the date
fixed, and the tickets and hotel rooms booked, the real fun begins. Now you will
have the opportunity to prepare a focused and engaging talk and the privilege
of entreating your colleagues to consider matters of interest and concern
originating from a perspective cultivated in your heart and mind. There are few
professional opportunities that equate to the thrill and honour of providing a
keynote address: to be, as Judith Ramaley (2000) describes it, "a learner among
learners willing to embrace the novel and unexpected and able to be an agent
of change". A keynote address is a significant opportunity to gain the immediate
feedback of your peers on your work, to transfer research knowledge to practice
knowledge, to debate and disseminate ideas, and to contribute to your field by
provoking action and inspiring further research in your discipline. In providing
a keynote address, one models scholarly practice and may encourage other
members of one's community to step up and engage, experiment and iterate,
prove or disprove, and expand the discipline or profession.

As academics, we tend to spend a preponderance of time working in solitary
study. "We prefer to conduct our own investigations on our own terms, with
conditions set by our own protocols and interests" (Ramaley, 2000), but
there is virtue and value in entering into a dialectic through preparing and
providing a keynote. It helps us to get out of our own heads and out of our own
immediate contexts. It provides opportunity to test the resonance and validity
of our assumptions and approaches with others equally steeped in their own
experiences and practices. It can also advance the thinking of our colleagues
who may be grappling with very similar quandaries of theory and practice and
will benefit from over-laying their context, experiences and knowledge with
what you present.

Conferences are effective at bringing people together to discuss emergent
themes, issues and possibilities and they offer the ability for participants to
share current thinking in its nascent form and without the lag associated with
the peer-review publication process so conferences can serve as wonderful
vehicles for moving projects forward. Conferences can also serve as rich venues
for significant collegial debate. Giroux (2013) celebrates conferences as public
gatherings where critical dialogue can be undertaken and where "intellectuals
have a responsibility to unsettle power, trouble consensus, and challenge
common sense". Conferences can serve as sites where social interactions
support engagement with novel perspectives ultimately leading to further
research, knowledge development, and advances in theory and practice.
Typically, conference organizing committee members have done their research

and have selected a compelling theme for the conference – one that will be of broad-based interest to potential conference participants. They have likely chosen to approach you to serve as a featured speaker because you have some demonstrated or documented history of leadership on the matter at hand. They will want you to share that perspective, knowledge and experience with the assembled conference participants in order to seed further conversations. A topical and trenchant keynote address can effectively promote conversations, but do not forget that opportunities to feed conversation both before and after the conference exist as well. As Friesen (2001) has noted, a conference actually has a pre-text or conversations around the theme that precede the provision of the conference gathering, and it is important to be tuned into those conversations so that your keynote will flow logically to and from them. Leading up to the conference and following it, consider taking advantage of conference social media channels to seed, cultivate and harvest ideas related to your chosen topic, and as an opportunity to connect with others who share your interests and may become valued collaborators. Keynote speakers, in choosing to engage deeply with current dilemmas and possibilities in the field, can contribute to the richness and productivity of a conference.

Indeed, keynote speakers have a pivotal role to play in ensuring the professional value of a conference for those in attendance. A good keynote speaker will not resort to providing a pre-packaged talk that is unrelated to the conference theme. Nor will a good keynote aim simply to affirm already well-established theories and practices a-critically. A good keynote speaker should not aim to placate; but rather, as Corey (2016) argues about the work of public intellectuals, be cognizant of audience, "not because she wishes to massage or assuage them, but because she wants to tear them apart. Her aim is to turn [her audience] from what they are into what they are not, to alienate [them] from themselves". It is the work of a keynote speaker to create shifts and rifts in the thinking of those in the room – and to make familiar ideas seem newly alien – through provocation, interrogation and the placing of intellectual demands upon those gathered together.

It is not, however, the role of the keynote speaker to befuddle the audience with highly theoretical jargon or baffle them with a disgorgement of data. Giroux (2013) and Ramaley (2000) among others warn about the perils of losing ground with your audience through speaking in highly technical or disciplinary language that will not be familiar or easily understandable by a wide range of audience members. Speaking as plainly and descriptively as possible will allow audience members to access the critical components of your arguments and insights more directly without first having to struggle through an interpretation of your word choice. When composing your keynote address, it may prove helpful to read it aloud frequently – either in isolation or to a private audience – checking for jargon and long, complex phrases that will leave both you and your audience breathless. If some technical language is required, define terms as best as possible and aim to ensure that your audience will be able to keep pace with your argument, but will not feel insulted by overly frequent reminders of the meaning of terms.

Keynote speakers should be similarly judicious in the selection of data and other forms of evidence they display. Making use of clean, appealing, and inoffensive visuals without much text on the slides can be an effective way to keep your audience engaged and build interest in your talk. On the other hand, attempting to persuade the audience through an examination of dense charts, graphs, or point form findings, projected in vanishingly small text on slides that are only viewable by those squinting in the front rows of the auditorium, is likely to lose more people than compel them to follow your argument. It is better to make limited use of such evidence in the slide deck designed to support the talk, and arrange to post a works-cited list on a commonly accessible site following the conference. Do remember, however, to cite any sources used, including open content, appropriately in the materials that you share visually or verbally before, during, or following your talk.

Once your talk has concluded, it may be possible to arrange for additional opportunities to engage in conversations during and following the conference gathering. If you are interested in formalizing arrangements for connecting with conference participants interested in further conversations, consult with the conference organizers to see if it would be possible to organize an additional conference presentation that would somehow serve as a complement to the keynote address, or an informal gathering of interested participants at a break, luncheon, or evening session. Even simply arranging to collect the business cards or email contact information of interested parties can provide a mechanism for sharing thinking and news of evolving practice and research, and work to ensure that the conversations will continue following the conclusion of the conference.

4   Reflection and Projection

After the conference, it is also good practice to seek an opportunity to receive feedback on your talk from the conference organizers and participants. You will benefit from considering what worked well and what did not prove as successful as you would have hoped in the delivery of your keynote address. The conference organizers may also seek feedback from you on your experience as a keynote speaker that will help them in organizing future events. This exchange of insights is valuable to ensuring high quality professional development in your community and can be undertaken successfully through formal or informal mechanisms, but is sufficiently important to your personal growth and development, as well as that of your colleagues that it is worth triggering such an exchange of feedback if the conference committee does not.

Finally, after a bit of time has passed following the conference, carve out a moment to reflect on your experience as a keynote speaker. Read through your talk again with a kind, but critical eye, and weigh it against the conversations had at the conference, the questions proffered by the audience, any recently published work of relevance, and your own evolved thinking on the subject matter. As Gross and Fleming (2011) teach us, "writing original papers for conferences is a vehicle for idea concretization in three senses: (1) it forces one to finally write up one's thoughts enough to stage a coherent oral performance; (2) the encouragement or discouragement that one receives from fellow panellists, commentators and audience members helps one determine whether a newly minted project is worth following through to completion; and (3) beyond mere encouragement or discouragement, the specific feedback an intellectual receives about their work in a conference setting may influence the future direction of that work" (p. 169).

Once your keynote address has been delivered, take some time to contemplate what you have learned through the unique opportunity to speak publicly and interact with important themes and possibilities with your colleagues. Consider changes you would make to the talk specifically, as well as what improvements you would make to the work of serving as a keynote speaker again in the future. It is also worth mulling over the prospect of converting your talk into a paper for a peer-review journal, either as a sole author or in partnership with some of the keen collaborators who enjoyed your talk and the conversation that extended beyond the conference.

A transformative keynote address should be sufficiently provocative and engaging to spur further conversation, research, and experimentation following the conference. The keynote speaker can sustain the engagement of conference participants with the critical theories and practices discussed by maintaining connections and encouraging on-going work. In this way, the effort taken to prepare and deliver the keynote address has lasting significance for the academic community and can deepen the rewards of committing to serve as a featured speaker.

References

Atherton, C. (2015). 'Very inflated rhetoric, polysyllables and so on': The public intellectual and jargon in the academy. *Media International Australia, 156*(1), 98–107.

Blumen, O., & Bar-Gal, Y. (2006). The academic conference and the status of women: The annual meetings of the Israeli geographical society. *The Professional Geographer, 58*(3), 341–355.

Corey, R. (2016, January). How intellectuals create a public. *Chronicle of Higher Education.* Retrieved from https://www.chronicle.com/article/How-Intellectuals-Create-a/234984

Friese, H. (2001). Thresholds in the ambit of discourse: On the establishment of authority at academic conferences. In P. Becker & W. Clark (Eds.), *Little tools of knowledge: Historical essays on academic and bureaucratic practices* (pp. 285–312). Ann Arbor, MI: University of Michigan Press.

Giroux, H. A. (2004). Cultural studies, public pedagogy, and the responsibility of intellectuals. *Communication and critical/cultural studies, 1*(1), 59–79.

Gross, N., & Fleming, C. (2011). Academic conferences and the making of philosophical knowledge. In C. Camic, N. Gross, & M. Lamont (Eds.), *Social knowledge in the making* (pp. 151–180). Chicago, IL: University of Chicago Press.

Kerber, L. K. (2008). Conference rules, part 2. *Chronicle of Higher Education, 54*(34), 1.

Ramaley, J. A. (2000). Change as a scholarly act: Higher education research transfer to practice. *New Directions for Higher Education, 2000*(110), 75–88.

Stanley, J. (1995). Pain(t) for healing: The academic conference and the classed/embodied self. In V. Walsh & L. Morley (Eds.), *Feminist academics: Creative agents for change* (pp. 169–182). London: Taylor & Francis.

PART 3

Organizing a Conference

∵

CHAPTER 7

Engendering Learning by Engaging Potential Participants through Conference Focus and Format

Celia Popovic and Alice L. E. V. Cassidy

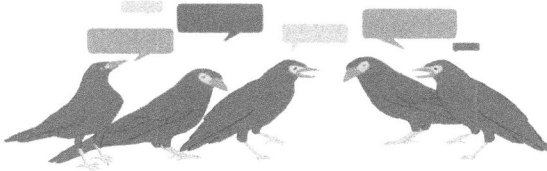

A number of years ago, while still a graduate student, I attended a well-known conference in New York City. On top of my excitement of travelling there, I was delighted to have had my paper accepted at such a prestigious forum. I recall strolling through the city on the way to the conference hotel (since there was no way I could afford to stay there) with my bag ever so casually draped over my shoulder, sporting my brown leather jacket, white scarf, aviator sunglasses, and my fancy take-out tea. I felt like I could conquer the world! I arrived at my session early to meet the session moderator like I had been coached to do as a good graduate student. I was informed that each presenter would have 20 minutes to share their work and that questions would be saved until the end. Being the last of four presenters I took comfort in knowing that I had the opportunity to listen and observe three much more experienced presenters before I was up. Maybe I could learn a thing or two on how to present at such a venue. Indeed I did learn a thing...or two. I learned that 20 minutes each is a guideline, not a rule. By the time the others had finished their presentations, I was left with eight minutes to complete my own. I came all the way to NYC on my own dime, for eight minutes and no questions.
       MANDY FRAKE-MISTAK

∵

1 Introduction

This chapter is designed for colleagues who are or soon will be designing a new conference, or taking on the organization and planning of a regularly scheduled conference. In both situations, you have a chance to make the event

© KONINKLIJKE BRILL NV, LEIDEN, 2018 | DOI 10.1163/9789004373013_007

memorable and effective for participants, presenters, sponsors and others involved. You will wish to avoid the situation faced in the anecdote above, through careful planning and management of the event.

In this chapter, we look at several aspects of conference format, through the lenses of learning and other benefits to participants. We will look at working with others (which may include guidelines and assistance from a representative of the society), including timelines, delegating tasks for team members and enlisting volunteers. Setting the schedule, promotions, registration, budgets and booking of space and food are also important. As the conference is about to start, important considerations include keeping momentum going, day-to-day logistics, surviving and enjoying the conference, greeting and networking with participants and dealing with the unexpected.

Chapter 8 provides focused detail about presentation formats; 9 gives guidance for ensuring an impact beyond the immediate conference. In 10 you will find a guide to using social media in conferences, and in Chapter 11 we review ways to evaluate a conference.

You are about to organize a conference, be it something brand new, an event you organize each year, or one that you host this year at your institution in concert with a society, the event moving to different location each year.

We argue that conferences should be regarded in a similar light to teaching. Although often treated as a different and separate activity from classroom or lecture based teaching the similarities are considerable. A presenter shares their knowledge about a topic with a group of others who are interested in the topic and who, between them, bring a range of backgrounds and level of prior knowledge. Knowing as we do, that active and experiential student-centred approaches engender long lasting and deep levels of learning (Biggs, 1999; Kolb, Boyatzis, & Mainemelis, 2000; Ramsden, 2003) why not apply this to conferences?

In a session entitled *Practicing what we preach*, one of us (Alice) and colleagues (Poole, Lee, Light, & Cassidy, 2008) focused on conference pedagogy. We used 16 Guidelines on learning from The University of New South Wales, crafted by Adrian Lee and Michele Scoufis (http://www.guidelinesonlearning.com/), each guideline defining an area of research about student learning. We asked participants to describe what an ideal conference looked like to them, noting similarities and differences between classroom and conference learning, with results contributed from 26 delegates (see full results at https://cassidyinview.wordpress.com/by-topic/conference-pedagogy-and-planning/results-from-a-conference-session-about-conference-pedagogy/). Building in example results from this activity with our own experiences and reflections, we have used the guidelines as a framework for considering conference formats through the lens of learning throughout this chapter.

These are the 16 guidelines:

1 Active Engagement: Effective learning is supported when students are *actively engaged* in the learning process at every stage.
2 Climate of inquiry: Effective learning is supported by a *climate of inquiry* where students feel appropriately challenged and activities are linked to research and scholarship.
3 Fun: Activities that are interesting and challenging, but which also create opportunities for students to have *fun*, can enhance the learning experience.
4 Reflection: Structured occasions for *reflection* allow students to explore their experiences, challenge current beliefs, and develop new practices and understandings.
5 Prior knowledge: Learning is more effective when students' *prior experience and knowledge* are recognised and built on.
6 Relevance: Students become more engaged in the learning process if they can see the *relevance* of their studies to professional, disciplinary and/or personal contexts, for example through linking learning experiences to the workplace or wider community.
7 Dialogue: If *dialogue* is encouraged between students and teachers and among students (in and out of class), thus creating a community of learners, student motivation and engagement can be increased.
8 Diversity: The educational experiences of all students are enhanced when the *diversity* of their experiences is acknowledged, valued and drawn on in learning and teaching approaches and activities.
9 Multiple modes: Students learn in different ways and their learning can be better supported by the use of *multiple* teaching methods and *modes* of instruction (visual, auditory, kinaesthetic and read/write).
10 Clear goals: Clearly articulated expectations, *goals*, learning outcomes and course requirements increase student motivation and improve learning.
11 Responsibility: When students are encouraged to take *responsibility* for their own learning, they are more likely to develop higher-order thinking skills, such as analysis, synthesis and evaluation and be better prepared for life-long learning.
12 Intentions: Graduate attributes – the qualities and skills the university hopes its students will develop as a result of their university studies – are most effectively acquired in a disciplinary context.
13 Technology: Learning can be enhanced and independent learning skills developed through *appropriate use of information and communication technologies*.

14 Learning co-operatively: *Learning co-operatively* with peers – rather than in an individualistic or competitive way – may help students develop interpersonal, professional and cognitive skills to a higher level.

15 Aligned assessment: Effective learning is facilitated by *assessment* practices and other student learning activities that are designed to support the achievement of desired learning outcomes.

16 Feedback: Meaningful and timely *feedback* to students improves learning.

Before applying each of these guidelines to a conference context, we begin with general guidance on organizing a conference.

First ask yourself, "Why would people attend?". As argued in Chapter 1, social contact or networking is a key reason that people attend conferences. Atzmueller, Doerfel, Hotho, Mitzlaff, and Stumme (2012) found that conference participants' face-to-face contacts and selection of sessions link to their particular communities, including special interest groups. Klein (1997) offers a tongue-in-cheek overview of how to get the most out of attending, noting, as way of summary:

> Finally, there is a school of thought that suggests that the maximum benefit from conferences is to be obtained by making copious notes from all the talks, seeking out delegates who are working in the same areas as you, comparing results, and discussing the latest developments in your field, culminating in a ritual exchange of e-mail addresses. This is dangerous heresy, and is to be avoided at all costs.

On deciding when to offer a conference, timing in the year may be up to your team, or set by the society with whom you work. The same might be true of the style, schedule specifics or other key conference details.

Chapter 4 described many popular and emerging session formats, and Chapter 8 looks at these from the perspective of a conference organizer. In this chapter we consider the overall design of the time together. In Campbell and Popovic's research project (see Introduction) respondents stated networking as the primary purpose for attending. This was supported by Cassidy and Simmons' poster session at EDC (2009) where 26 contributors noted what they thought characterizes the 'best ever' conference experiences. Both Campbell and Popovic and Cassidy and Simmons found the two most common elements were related to time and space (15) and interactivity or active engagement (14). The message from both explorations is clear: people want plenty of time to network and to be offered varied ways to talk with one another. This could involve frequent lengthy breaks between sessions, a welcoming atmosphere at meals and receptions, and that everyone feels included, especially those new to the conference. Cassidy and Simmons found that while a fifth of respondents suggested removing concurrent sessions, the rest did not mention this. Campbell and Popovic's respondents voiced discontent with sessions that failed to do as they promised, including engaging participants and linking to the conference theme. We will discuss these issues in more detail in Chapter 8.

When organizing a conference, even a one-day local event, it is rare for one person to do it all; much more commonly it is a team effort. The team may be from one or multiple institutions. For a comprehensive list of conference tasks, see https://cassidyinview.wordpress.com/by-topic/conference-pedagogy-and-planning/conference-task-list/. When the conference is the regular event of a society, there are usually guidelines and assistance available from a representative of the society. See http://www.stlhe.ca/affiliated-groups/educational-developers-caucus/edc-conferences/ for examples.

Here we offer some advice on working together and identify the key priorities.

1.1   *Working Together*
The key to a well-organized and smooth-running conference is to ensure that the team involved has a clear idea of what needs to be done, when and by whom.

1.2   *Delegating Team Members for Particular Jobs*
Colleagues who comprise organizing and planning committees offer a wealth of experience, interests and the time they can commit. Regular meetings, co-created task lists, and timelines not only keep everyone on track, but sets a positive tone for the event to come. We suggest one person is tasked with sending updates about who has signed up for which tasks, and keeps track of progress.

1.3   *Enlisting Volunteers*
Conferences often make use of volunteers. These are often students, but may include staff or faculty. One way to raise the profile of volunteers is for them to wear the same colour T-shirt, as they direct conference participants at the venue and provide general information. Remember to thank volunteers both publically and privately. Most commonly a thank you is made during the closing plenary, and volunteers are given a small gift (and/or the chance to attend a few sessions without paying registration) and/or letter acknowledging their participation.

1.4   *Peer Review of Proposals*
The peer review process is pivotal to a well-organized and highly attended conference. The aim of the peer review process is to ensure a high quality

of sessions that are aligned with the conference aims. Many participants are eligible for funding to attend only if their peer-reviewed proposal is accepted. Thus it is important to ensure a fair and relevant peer review process.

The peer review should result in the selection of the most appropriate sessions chosen from the proposals. Obviously the larger the number of proposals the more rigorous the process will need to be. Peer reviewers should be encouraged to provide feedback to authors to enable them to improve the session and its description, either to clarify issues for this conference, or to assist them with future proposals.

Ideally aim to have 2 to 3 volunteer reviewers for each proposed session. Recruit sufficient reviewers so that no one reviewer is overloaded. Overload results in superficial reviewing as the reviewer may not have time to give full consideration to each proposal. It is preferable to have a mix of folks new to the process and those who have reviewed for that conference in the past. Provide reviewers with clear guidelines, just as you would if you had multiple graders marking students' work. These guidelines are likely to include such questions as: Does the description align with the conference aims? Is the proposal well written, clear, and relevant?

Peer review is a great way to involve colleagues who might not attend the conference, but can still play an important role in shaping what is offered. Being a reviewer can help one feel 'part of it' and also help to create better proposals in the future, by reviewers and presenters alike.

1.5   *Financial Considerations*

A balanced budget is as important as schedules, timelines, and guidelines. This will determine how much to charge for registration, for members and non-members if appropriate, and how much to spend on promotions, meals and so on. If you are arranging a conference on behalf of a society, make sure all parties are clear as to who is responsible for collecting fees and paying bills. Agree what will happen in the case that the conference makes a profit or a loss. For example, the EDC has a contingency fund available to cover costs to hosts should an event have to be cancelled due to weather or other unexpected occurrences out of their control. Any profit is shared equally between the host institution and the society.

1.6   *Sustainability*

There are a number of ways to ensure your conference has as little impact on the environment as possible. Some relate to your budget but many do not. Consider if you need a unique conference bag. Your institution's bookstore might provide one at no charge. If the conference is a regular event (associated with a society or not), can you provide a one-time bag that registrants are encouraged to bring back in subsequent years? This can prevent bag overload by participants, save money and resources, and create a conference or society identity. Can the 'swag', (which might include local information, donated items such as pens to help advertise, and other material) be laid out at the registration table such that delegates choose what they want rather than throw out unwanted materials. Do you need 'swag' at all?

Where at all possible, avoid the use of disposable dishes, cups, cutlery and containers (the box lunch is famous for this!) Otherwise see which materials can be recycled or composted. Clearly marked containers and a brief announcement about it can go a long way in reducing landfill. Add a 'bring your own coffee mug' note on the conference website. Some people may even bring their own reusable cutlery and plate.

We now return to the 16 guidelines on learning from the University of New South Wales, and address each of them from the perspective of a conference organizer.

2   Active Engagement

As with teaching, conferences are more likely to result in learning if the participants are actively engaged. A similarity between classroom and conference learning is the experiential aspect; being active and interactive provides opportunities for 'comparing notes' among learners, helping to reflect on what was learned and how to proceed from here (Poole et al., 2008). When designing a conference, consider which formats and structure are most likely to engage participants. For instance, think about offering multiple sessions with smaller groups, rather than keeping the whole group contained in a lecture theatre throughout the entire event. All too often, one-day events in particular tend to rely on corralling participants in one room, much like some courses require students to attend lectures in large halls without the opportunity for smaller groups which are more conducive to engaged discussion. Most multi-day conferences have a mix of plenaries and concurrent sessions and it could be argued that the former are usually overly didactic. Having said that, we have experienced very active and lively keynotes and other plenary sessions at conferences. We argue this should be more common. We can all think of engaging keynotes, as well as those that were less successful. See Chapter 6 for more discussion of keynotes.

3   Climate of Inquiry

When selecting keynote speakers and reviewing presentations think about the likely participants at the conference. How can you ensure that everyone will feel challenged (in a good way!) by the event? For example, identify the likely level of knowledge on the theme and pitch the call for the sessions to meet the needs of the widest group. We have attended some conferences where the pitch was wrong. Assuming participants are more knowledgeable and familiar with a theme than they are can be as bad as the reverse. If the conference is a precursor to some intended change, for example, to introduce a new approach to teaching, put yourself in the participants' shoes. What do they need to think about in order to open their minds to the proposed change? How can you engage them in a spirit of inquiry, rather than expect them to be passive recipients of new ideas? See the section below about learning cooperatively for an example where the conference theme of inquiry was built into a networking opportunity for conference delegates.

4   Fun

How can you make the conference fun without being overly gimmicky? This can be a matter of opinion and balance. According to Maslow's hierarchy of needs (Maslow, 1943) human beings need to have physical and safety needs met before they can begin to engage intellectually. It is not coincidental that organizers give attention to meals and refreshment arrangements. Since everyone needs to be 'fed and watered', conference meals and breaks are a non-negotiable element. However, these are also prime opportunities to play with expectations and introduce elements of fun without detracting from the seriousness of the sessions and keynotes.

If the conference is held at a warm time of year it may be appropriate to offer a barbecue lunch, allowing people to network informally out in the sunshine. Presenting food as a picnic can also work, as can introducing an element of surprise in the style of cuisine.

Think about the location: is it possible to link the conference with the environs? SEDA (Staff and Educational Development Association) conferences in recent years have made conscious attempts to do this, for example, including a tour of the Scottish Parliament building at Holyrood when the conference was held in Edinburgh, and the Millennium Stadium when in Cardiff. See Chapter 8 for further ideas around involving the environment. While you will wish to maintain an appropriate level of seriousness and intellectual engagement, it is possible to achieve this while also encouraging levity at times. One of us (Alice), when about to introduce the conference organizers at a one-day event, found herself with laryngitis. Instead of turning the job over to another, she used charades to introduce them. It was not only effective, but resulted in laughter and applause.

5 Reflection

Those participants who have taken our advice in Chapter 2 will make sure they reflect on their experience. However, most people benefit from a structured reminder to do so. All too often a conference can feel like an assault on the senses as we are over-stimulated with ideas and little chance for reflection. Boud, Keogh, and Walker (1985) describe reflection in the context of learning as those intellectual and affective activities in which individuals explore their experiences in order to lead to new understandings and appreciations. There are many ways to do this, such as to invite participants at regular intervals to think about one thing they will commit to on return to their 'day job'. Consider building reflection into the closing; see one example at https://cassidyinview.wordpress.com/by-topic/conference-pedagogy-and-planning/reflective-conference-closing-activity/

6 Prior Knowledge

Is it safe to assume that all participants will come to the conference with the same pertinent knowledge? It is not uncommon for conferences that are held by societies to be criticized for being cliquey. This is a criticism we have heard even though the societies themselves aim to be inclusive and welcoming. Consider the experience from the perspective of someone who has not attended before. Are there assumptions that are made by 'old hands', that may need to be made explicit for newcomers. The worst thing to hear from those attending for the first or second time is that the conference is cliquey. Inviting people into the network can take many forms. See what works best for your particular event.

Some conference organizers build in networking and familiarization sessions. Both EDC and SEDA, for example, invite new people to attend a session where a senior, experienced member of the community has breakfast with those who are attending for the first time, and answers their questions. STLHE invites student participants, both undergraduate and graduate, to a special event just before the main opening reception. This is an approach that can be adapted for annual in-house conferences.

7 Relevance

Consult with a range of people before deciding on your conference theme. A theme that may seem highly appropriate to some may feel exclusive to others. This can happen with conferences that are aimed at members of an institution just as much as it can happen with international conferences. If you aim to attract the widest audience, ensure that the conference sounds appealing to all.

If your conference takes place each year, it is most likely that you will see the usual crowd. But perhaps you want to attract people new to the conference. If you are hosting an internal conference, give thought to the ways you might attract attention, especially for its first few years.

If this is an annual conference for a particular organization be sure to include information about the forthcoming conference on the organization's website. The Educational Developers Caucus (EDC), for example, describes what its conference is and who it is for http://www.stlhe.ca/affiliated-groups/educational-developers-caucus/edc-conferences/.

Consider ways to spread the word to attract participation. Electronic means such as a website and emails are the most common. This includes regular reminders on host society and other listservs, and cross postings to other lists hosted by similar organizations in other countries. Use the various stages of conference organization as opportunities to promote the conference. This also serves to balance keeping the event in peoples' minds but not overwhelming them. Make new posts and announcements when information such as when keynote speakers are confirmed or the conference programme has been updated as well as when registration deadlines are coming up.

Electronic communication can be very effective for some, but do not rely on it as the sole marketing avenue. If someone does not respond immediately to an email they may overlook it. Repetition and overlap are good in this context. If you have an internal daily or weekly newspaper or newsletter use it to promote the conference.

Word of mouth and short announcements at events where prospective participants are likely to attend can help attract participants. The use of hard copy advertising is worth the expense. To save paper (and trees) give out bookmarks. Ask colleagues to post flyers in their own faculties and departments, as they will know where people are most likely to see them.

8   Dialogue

Some conferences such as at SEDA actively encourage if not insist on presenters indicating the way in which participants will engage in their sessions. We know that discussion is important for learning (Vygotsky, 1987); it is equally important for engagement in any social environment. When planning the conference, how can you maximise opportunities for participants to talk with each other, with presenters and with the keynote speakers? If you provide a conference banquet, are there ways to enhance engagement aside from the opportunity to speak with people on the same table?

Offer sign-up sheets for free evenings, either by topic or by restaurant, to enable people to meet others in informal settings. Organizers of the EDC conference have experimented with providing a dedicated block on the schedule to suggest a topic of discussion and/or sign-up, then those interested could go for a walk, coffee, or sit in a quiet corner to chat with others.

9   Diversity

Unless it is made explicit that there is a range of experience, participants may assume that they share common perspectives. Just as student learning is improved when diversity of background, culture, expectations, and needs are acknowledged, the same is true for conference participants. For example, it may be helpful to inform the keynote speaker about the likely make up of participants, particularly if they are not a member of your institution or of the society holding the conference. For instance, we have been to conferences in the past where the keynote speaker was not appreciated by a large proportion of the audience because the speaker pitched the talk incorrectly for them while being completely on the money for the others.

10   Multiple Modes

In the same way that learners benefit from hearing and seeing the same information in a variety of ways, how can you provide a similar experience for conference participants? Poole et al. (2008) report that delegates want to hear many points of view, including the knowledge and expertise of those who know more than they do, in both conference and classroom settings.

Chapter 8 discusses ideas on a range of session formats. Consider ways to provide a similar range of experience in other elements of the conference.

11   Clear expectations and Goals

We know it is important to set clear expectations and goals in our teaching (Cassidy, Nabavii, & Sipos, 2008); this applies just as much to conferences (Poole et al., 2008). What are the goals for the conference and for individual sessions? Do you need to make these explicit? Participants are often faced with choices between multiple attractive sounding sessions. Help them to make informed choices by providing clear abstracts for each session; some programmes indicate the proportion of time in each session that will be devoted to one-way, interaction, Q and A and other techniques. Colour-coding or labelling sessions by sub-theme can also help delegates decide which to attend.

Many conference sessions include a volunteer or member of the organizing committee at each session. Their tasks can include helping with technology, introducing speakers, turning late-comers away (if the room is full or for another reason to keep the session running smoothly), asking participants to complete a brief feedback form for presenters and so on.

A chief task is keeping the session on time, by giving the presenter time signals and making sure they adhere to them. This is most important in such sessions as described by the anecdote at the start of this chapter. Grouped papers can prove frustrating for presenters as their papers are often cheek by jowl with others, and unless well-moderated, timing can be a huge issue. However, if properly chaired, it can all go smoothly when multiple presenters are part of one session. Each presenter has a set amount of time, either with questions immediately after, or after all presenters are done. It is particularly important in these situations for a moderator to keep time and stop each speaker in turn when their time is up. This avoids each subsequent speaker having less and less time.

12   Responsibility

Consider how you could encourage participants to take responsibility for their own learning, aside from encouraging them to read Section 1 of this book! The format of some conferences encourages participants to behave like passive consumers. Alternatively, building in activities, engagement and reflection, as described earlier, is more likely to empower participants to take responsibility for their conference experience.

The SOLSTICE and CLT (Centre for Learning and Teaching) conference at Edge Hill University in 2017 included a 'Twalk', combining a walk with the use of Twitter. In this case it took the form of an organized walk around campus with prearranged stops at key learning related sites, such as a communal area, a computer lab, a lecture theatre, a teaching room. As they arrived at each stop participants were encouraged to Tweet (using Twitter) responses to location related questions. The added twist to this was that participants were invited from other locations around the world. This required some prearranging on the part of the distant locations as they had to design a walk taking in similar locations at the same time intervals. One of us (Celia) successfully joined the UK hosts from her location in Toronto, Canada.

13   Conference Intentions

At first glance, the guideline regarding graduate attributes may not seem appropriate for conferences. However, if we think of this in terms of the overall intention of the conference it has greater resonance. Having decided on a theme for the conference, be sure that the constituent parts, the keynote, the sessions, the ambiance, all align with the intent. For example, in a conference focusing on problem-based learning, be sure to include aspects of PBL in the design, instead of just talking about it.

The very memorable 2005 STLHE conference hosted by the University of Prince Edward Island had its theme, *The Student Experience of Learning*, built into many aspects of the event. These included students leading an interactive opening session, a student-style backpack (that one of us still uses regularly), a daily newsletter created by students, and students as co-presenters in many of the concurrent sessions. Talk about walking the talk!

14   Appropriate Use of Technology and Social Media

See Chapter 10 for guidance on using social media in conferences. Technology is wider than the use of social media. Make sure the presenters are able to make best use of technology, bearing in mind that some venues bring particular challenges. Be clear with presenters regarding expectations. For example, do they merely need to bring their presentation on a memory stick, or are they expected to bring their own laptops? Is it possible to enable those who cannot attend in person to join using an online conferencing application, or is the wifi too weak to rely on this?

15   Learning Co-Operatively

What are some options to do this? With a theme of Inquiry at the 2002 STLHE hosted by McMaster University, participants had an option to sign up for one of several inquiry groups. Meetings were dispersed throughout the conference schedule, during some breakfasts, lunches and late afternoons. They were planned to take place so as not to conflict with the 'main schedule' of events, joining one group with the same participants, led by a facilitator, was an excellent way to meet like-minded colleagues and work on a topic of mutual interest.

16   Aligned Assessment

How often do we include any kind of assessment in a conference? Although unusual, it may be that the metaphor of conferences as learning gives us pause to consider whether it should. Many conference attendees comment on the experience of hearing a great number of interesting ideas and approaches, and leaving with the full intention to implement them in their home institution. But a month or two later and they are struggling to recall what it was that was so impressive at the time. In Chapter 11 we discuss the issue of maximizing learning through evaluation and feedback, and will revisit this issue there.

17   Meaningful and Timely Feedback

See Chapter 11 for advice on ways to collect kinds of feedback and other data in order to evaluate the conference effectively.

17.1   *During the Conference*
After months of planning and hours of work, eventually and inevitably the first day of the conference will arrive. The work does not end here, instead the focus shifts.

17.2   *Keeping Momentum Going*
Just before the conference begins, bring together as many of the organizing team as you can, or walk around and chat with them individually. Failing this, send emails out the evening before. Thank everyone for their work so far and tell them what a great event this is going to be, that it would not be happening without their energy. Make this sincere and personalized. Tell yourself the same things! It can be all too easy to say "Phew" and relax, but this is the time to keep energy levels up, a smile on your face, and find ways to keep everyone around you energized and excited for what is to come.

18   Greeting Participants and Networking

Whether people are coming to the conference you have organized for the first or the fifteenth time, they have put a lot of time, effort and money into attending, be they a presenter or a participant. Find ways to welcome them. Here are some examples:

Include a special note in their registration package and/or in their accommodation if everyone is staying in the same location.

Post a welcome banner at the conference venue, and if possible, welcome signs at the hotels or institution residences where you know people are staying.

Offer a buddy system. This can come into effect as people arrive, or be arranged in advance. The 2016 POD Network conference http://podnetwork.org/event/2016-pod-network-conference/organized a buddy sign-up list, where folks new to the conference could pair with those who had attended before.

Ensure that name badges are easy to read from a short distance away. The first name may be printed in larger font than the rest. Consider printing names on both sides of the badge (they twirl around sometimes). Though the conference logo is usually on name badges, it should not take up too much room; after all, everyone knows what conference they are at! As badges are given out, ask people to adjust the string so it sits at an appropriate level for people to see.

Several conferences have made use of ribbons that are added to the bottom of the tag, such as 'first time at this conference', 'organizing committee', or 'peer reviewer'. You might even consider other headings, such as discipline or teaching technique, or even something a bit more playful that people can choose from, such as 'cyclist', 'avid gardener', 'loves cilantro' to help break the ice when networking. If you do not wish to use (or do not have the budget for) commercially produced labels you can achieve much the same result using sticky labels and pens and invite participants to decorate their labels as they see fit. The purpose of this is to make it easier for people to engage in small talk to break the ice before entering into more engaging discussions.

18.1   Day-to-Day Logistics

In the planning stage, tasks were set for all organizing team members and volunteers. Make sure there are people 'signed' up to take on the array of small and larger jobs on a day to day basis once the conference is underway. This can help keep things moving smoothly if (or when) the unexpected occurs.

18.2   Dealing with the Unexpected

When one of us (Alice) directed the UBC Shad Valley Program (an intense 4-weeks and full days mix of science, technology and entrepreneurship for high-school students), we had a saying, after months of planning work, on the eve before the 52 students and 10 staff all showed up: "The train has left the station!" You cannot go back and fix something you wished you had done (or not done!). What you can do now is address issues as they arise; sometimes no one could have predicted them. If you know you will run this conference again, keep notes. Ask the calmest members of the team to be on hand to 'put out fires'. Fix things if you can. Deal and move on. Harking back to the programme just described, the job of one member of the staff was to place an order for about 100 baseball caps, on which the programme name was embroidered, and pick them up. She called me, distraught: "The caps all say Shade Valley!! What do I do?" I thought about it for a moment then asked her, "Can you ask them to take the E out?" She arrived a few hours later with perfect caps for us to give out.

18.3   *Surviving and Enjoying the Conference*

Once the conference is underway, give yourself time and space to enjoy it. All the planning is done. You have systems in place to deal with the unexpected. The conference, be it a single day or multiple days, will go by so much sooner than you ever thought possible. You will even maybe feel a bit sad once it is all over. Our advice is don't sweat the small stuff, and enjoy it. Be sure to take part yourself and make sure all members of the team do so too.

References

Atzmueller, M., Doerfel, S., Hotho, A., Mitzlaff, F., & Stumme, G. (2012). Face-to-face contacts at a conference: Dynamics of communities and roles. In M. Atzmueller, A. Chin, D. Helic, & A. Hotho (Eds.), *Modeling and mining ubiquitous social media: Lecture notes in computer science* (Vol. 7472, pp. 21–39). Berlin: Springer-Verlag.

Biggs, J. (1999). *Teaching for quality learning at university*. Buckingham: Open University Press.

Boud, D., Keogh, R., & Walker, D. (1985). Promoting reflection in learning: A model. In D. Boud, R. Keogh, & D. Walker (Eds.), *Reflection: Turning experience into learning* (pp. 18–40). London: Kogan Page.

Boule, M. (2011). *Mob rule learning: Camps, unconferences, and trashing the talking head*. Retrieved from http://chronicle.com/blogs/wiredcampus/q-a-a-onetime-librarian-talks-about-the-unconference-movement/34434?sid=at&utmsource=at&utm_medium=en

Cassidy, A., Nabavii, M., & Sipos, Y. (2008). Learning objectives and objectives. In Y. Harlap (Ed.), *Road to global citizenship: An educators' toolbook*. Vancouver: Centre for Teaching and Academic Growth, in Collaboration with UNICEF, and University of British Columbia. Retrieved from http://wiki.ubc.ca/Documentation:CTLT_programs/Global_Citizenship/Road_to_Global_Citizenship

Cassidy, A. L. E. V., & Simmons, N. (2009, February). *Conference pedagogy: Change can be good.* Educational Developers Caucus Conference, Durham College, Oshawa.

Harrison, R. (2010). Unique benefits of conference attendance as a method of professional development for LIS professionals. *The Serials Librarian, 59*(3–4), 263–270. Retrieved from http://www.tandfonline.com/doi/full/10.1080/0361526X.2010.489353

Klein, P. (1997). How to succeed at conferences. *Physics World, 10*(1), 68. Retrieved from http://iopscience.iop.org/article/10.1088/2058–7058/10/1/35

Kolb, D., Boyatzis, R. E., & Mainemelis, C. (2000). Experiental learning theory: Previous research and new direction. In R. J. Sternberg & L. Zhang (Eds.), *Perspectives on cognitive, learning, and thinking styles.* Mahwah, NJ: Lawrence Erlbaum.

Maslow, A. H. (1943). A theory of human motivation. *Psychological Review, 50*(4), 370–396.

Poole, G., Lee, A., Light, G., & Cassidy, A. (2008, October). *Practicing what we preach: Applying evidence-based guidelines to conference pedagogy.* International Society for the Scholarship of Teaching and Learning (ISSOTL) Conference, University of Alberta, Edmonton.

Ramsden, P. (2003). *Learning to teach in higher education* (2nd ed., p. 47). London: Routledge.

Vygotsky, L. (1987). *Collected works* (Vol. 1). New York, NY: Plenum.

CHAPTER 8

Ensuring Learning through Session Formats and Networking Opportunities

Fiona Campbell and Celia Popovic

Its 10.00am. Your conference is about to commence. You hear the growing buzz of greetings and conversation as delegates begin to arrive. You sense their keen anticipation and their thirst for the experiences that lie ahead – and for the welcoming coffee. You are quaking ever so slightly at the potential derailment scenarios playing through your head but largely you feel a warm glow of assurance because you know that the programme you hold in your hand will enable your delegates to learn, develop, and grow. You know it includes sessions with interesting content and varied formats that will inspire. You know that the networking opportunities will stimulate delegates to share their practice, and perhaps, in future, to co-author or collaborate together and form long-lasting professional friendships. You know it is going to be a good conference. But just how did you get to here?

1   Introduction

This chapter aims to empower you to create a programme of sessions and opportunities that energise participants, engender learning, and impact practice, to create a programme that, in Simmons' words (2010), kindles 'intellectual community and reinvigorates'. The nature and format of the sessions and networking opportunities that make up a conference are often critical for learning to take place and our focus here will be on these and on ensuring that learning emanates from them.

In this chapter, we quote from the research we did (detailed in the Introduction) investigating participants' perspectives regarding conference sessions and networking opportunities. We will hear the voices of the conference participants themselves saying what made the difference for them in terms of their learning, their practice, and potentially that of their colleagues and organisations. Hearing the words of the approximately 200 participants across the world who contributed their views to our research will be valuable in helping you consider how best to provide for the different aspirations, needs and preferences of those attending your conference. For each of these perspectives we will then discuss what to do to enhance the experience for conference participants.

The chapter will first consider conference formats discussing a range of possible approaches for plenaries and parallel sessions and the pros and cons of each in terms of their suitability in engendering learning.

The chapter will then consider networking opportunities and discuss the practicalities of how to enable formal and informal networking opportunities in your conference. We aim to help you steer that tricky course between being too heavy-handed and too hands-off in order to achieve that light touch which will generate purposeful, engaging and, ultimately, rewarding, networking among your conference participants.

2   Conference Sessions: What Do Participants Want?

In our research on the impact of conferences on practice (see Introduction) we asked those taking part about the sessions they had attended in particular conferences which they believed would enable change in their individual practice or that of their organization. We then asked them what made the difference in terms of the:

– content of sessions
– nature of the delivery of sessions
– contributions of other delegates in sessions

and we'll now look at each of these in turn.

2.1   *Content of Sessions*
The survey respondents listed the following as the attributes which made the most difference:

– Relevant
– Innovative
– Developmental
– Of practical use

They also told us what didn't work.

2.1.1   Relevant

Relevance is the most highly valued attribute. Unfortunately, it can also be the most personal since it includes relevance to many things: to the participant as an individual, their role, their institution, and forthcoming changes. It also relates to academic relevance particularly in relation to their own scholarship or professional experience.

Our participants indicated they want:

> Knowledge gained directly relevant to practice.

> Relevant, interesting, well-presented.

> Clear presentation of a dilemma we are facing at my institution too and a practical demonstration on how they solved that dilemma. I could immediately see how to apply that in my own institution.

What to Do about This

Since relevance is in the eye of the beholder, this can be a difficult aspect to judge. We believe though, that this is best addressed at the planning stage and in the peer review process. We discuss planning and peer review in the previous chapter, but for now be mindful of the aims of the conference, the likely needs of the participants and the need to align this with the session formats. For example, if the conference aim is to bring about some sort of change in an institution, it is likely to be more successful if participants are given the opportunity to discuss issues in some detail, than if they are presented with a one-way flow of information. If the purpose of the conference is to share research findings, then the sessions need to be designed to enable multiple presentations with sufficient time to convey the key information.

2.1.2   Innovative

Innovation is significant including a focus on innovative practices and approaches or something new: ideas, insights, research, tools, concepts, information.

> Meeting people who use innovative strategies.

Really useful introduction to a range of tools – some of which I had not come across.

Good combination of the confirmatory – how strong we are and how innovative – to draw us, re-energised, on our journey.

What to Do about This
What is innovative for some may be 'old hat' for others. Use your contacts to identify the innovators in your community and invite them to take part in the conference. For instance, if this is an institutional conference approach the award winners, the early adopters, and the champions and encourage them to share their good practice. They may be unaware that their work is innovative. Consider some of the active sessions suggested later, such as 'maker space' to encourage participants to try out new tools in a safe environment.

2.1.3   Developmental
Sessions which made a difference for respondents' own development were appreciated especially where they were thought-provoking or challenging.

Provocative and interesting sessions challenged us to think differently.

Inspiring. Full of new ideas to support my staff development and to encourage risk-taking.

What to Do about This
Use the conference as an opportunity to challenge and provoke colleagues' thinking. The 'un-conference' and panel presentations lend themselves to this approach.

2.1.4   Of Practical Use
Sessions that were practical were also popular and especially where respondents could see how they could adopt, adapt, and apply what they had learned to their own context. They also appreciated resources being provided, some of which they were able to use to effect change in their own contexts.
  Our participants commented on:

Grounded practical approach to a real problem.

Practical applicable ideas.

Practical approach, potential for impact on practice.

Fantastic examples of high quality resources available.

Interesting as it involved relating theory to practice.

What to Do about This
In the call for proposals and the review process encourage presenters to provide handouts and to share their presentation resources after the conference.

What They Did Not Appreciate
Respondents advised that they didn't appreciate sessions that lacked depth, new ideas or inspiration, were too abstract or did not move beyond personal opinions, or where presenters seemed to be using the session for themselves, for instance, to gather data for their own research or project.

2.2   Nature of Delivery of Sessions
The survey respondents listed the following as the attributes which made the most difference:

– Delivery
– Professionalism and experience of presenter
– Good time management
– Awareness of audience
– Interactivity, opportunity for questions and discussion

2.2.1   Delivery
Clarity was mentioned many times by respondents who also listed the importance of good presentation skills, and a presentation that was crisp, well structured, well-paced.

Strong, sparky presentation style and communicated key points very effectively.

Great ideas, well presented. Very thought-provoking, excellent examples.

Enjoyed the inspiring and charismatic speakers who made well-balanced arguments.

Well-researched and thoughtfully analysed.

What to Do about This
If this is an internal conference consider offering preparation sessions for presenters. This must be handled sensitively of course, as some seasoned academics may not take kindly to the suggestion that this is needed. For an external conference, provide guidance notes explaining what people appreciate and the dos and don'ts of how to achieve that.

2.2.2   Professionalism and Experience of Presenter
Respondents wanted the presenter to be knowledgeable, convincing – and enthusiastic.

> Clear and passionate.

> Brilliantly well-informed.

> Very exciting and impressive – fired people up.

> Another important attribute was that presenters spoke from experience:

> The personal stories of the presenter gave the topic a richness of meaning.

What to Do about This
Keep this in mind when inviting proposals and in the peer review process.

2.2.3   Good Time Management
This was important to respondents as it meant there were opportunities for them to interact, take part in discussion, ask questions and get to their next session – sometimes after a comfort break or via the coffee machine – on time!

> Included time to explore implications for our work.

> An excellent speaker and finished bang on time.

What to Do about This
If there are sufficient volunteers available, allocate an assertive time keeper to each session and ensure timings are enforced. Start on time and refuse to allow one presenter to take up more than their allocated spot.

2.2.4   Awareness of Audience
Respondents felt sessions were of most value where the presenter was familiar with the knowledge, experience and concerns of those participating.

Very informal session taking into consideration the audience experience and problems they encounter.

Very inclusive.

Included the participants well.

What to Do about This
Encourage participation in the conference description. Consider providing explicit guidance to presenters on what leads to success. You could also draw on our research to provide evidence.

2.2.5   Interactivity, Opportunity for Questions and Discussion
Activity and interactivity were very much appreciated by our respondents. They liked the opportunity to air their views, discuss ideas, engage in meaningful and purposeful activities, to ask questions and to have them answered.

[Valued] discussion is small groups.

Really useful table chats.

Questions picked up on useful points and were well answered.

The presenter allowed any questions no matter how trivial the person thought they were. He also offered his expertise…I was impressed by this generosity.

Lots of opportunities to ask questions.

Friendly, approachable open lecturer who actively asked questions and used current knowledge to answer questions and develop discussion.

What to Do about This
As with previous points, include advice about this on the conference website at the time the call is made for submissions and provide guidance with examples for presenters.

What They Did Not Appreciate
Respondents advised they didn't appreciate sessions where presenters were not aware of their audience, where there was no interactivity or use of engaging

methods, or there was no time for discussion and time management generally was poor.

2.3   *Contributions from Participation of Other Delegates in Sessions*

This part relates to the contribution of other participants in conference sessions rather than in the contributions to mutual learning resulting from networking.

The survey respondents listed the following as the attributes which made the most difference in sessions:

– Exchange of ideas and experiences and the sharing of concerns and solutions
– Opportunity to receive reassurance about own practice
– Chance to gain new perspectives.

2.3.1   Exchange of Ideas and Experiences and the Sharing of Concerns and Solutions

Respondents valued the opportunity for learning with other conference participants through exchange and sharing.

> Conferences are about interaction and exchange; face to face contact to share ideas and issues.

> Wide collection of views and experiences shared constructively.

> Sharing of useful ideas and experiences sets in motion future possible collaborations with previously unknown colleagues.

What to Do about This

Be sure to include multiple opportunities for discussion and networking in the schedule. Remind participants to reflect when in plenary. As we discussed in Chapter 7, the principles of good teaching can also apply to conferences. Participants, like students, may benefit from regular reminders to apply what they learn at the conference to their situation back at their institution.

2.3.2   Opportunity to Receive Reassurance about Own Practice

Some respondents explained how contributions from other participants at conferences mitigated against the solitary nature of the academic profession

> To realise you are not alone.

Opportunity to share ideas and find out what is happening elsewhere [which] helps to prevent silo thinking.

What to Do about This
Encourage participants to contribute actively to conference sessions and for presenters to share their presentation resources after the conference.

2.3.3   Chance to Gain New Perspectives
This was especially valued if it was from others who may be further down the road with implementation.

Great examples and some sharing of the difficulties in getting there.

[Appreciated   the   opportunity]   to   benchmark   practice   and see how others had overcome challenges and the encouragement to have a go!

What to Do about This
Be confident that your conference call will attract a wide range of responses ensuring a conference full of varied ideas and approaches.

What They Did Not Appreciate
Participants advised they did not appreciate irrelevant or tangential questions being asked which did not contribute to learning. They were particularly irritated by questioners who asked hostile questions designed to shoot down presenters or who used this opportunity to hold the floor for an overly-long time expounding their own views.

3   **Conference Plenaries: Maximizing Impact**

In this section, we will look at the nature and formats of plenary sessions that involve all the participants simultaneously and include keynote addresses.
    In each of the parts we will look at options and at the practicalities of planning to achieve the outcome and impact you want for your participants.

3.1   *Plenary Sessions*

3.1.1   Openings and Keynotes
There are a number of ways to open a conference as we touched on in the previous chapter. Whatever you choose as your opening, aim to use it to get

your conference off to an excellent start and to create the energy you – and your participants – want:

Participants said:

> Very positive vibe!

> A buzzing atmosphere.

3.1.2   Opening Keynote

As we discuss in Chapters 6 and 7, keynotes are the most usual way that conferences start and they provide an opportunity to create early interest and excitement among participants and hopefully a sense of satisfaction as they realise that yes, they definitely ARE in the right place! An excellent keynote can set the tone for the conference, address the issues uppermost on most participants' agenda – and inspire.

> Fantastic to have such a dynamic start to the conference, really made me positive about the rest of it.

A good keynote will have several qualities: their knowledge of the area is obvious but equally important is their ability to engage an audience and to speak convincingly and compellingly. The signs that a keynote has been excellent is the buzz of participants as they leave the plenary room and the number of times in the sessions and discussions that follow that their words are referenced. You can also expect positive evaluative comments:

> Excellent speaker and very motivating, energetic and inspiring.

> The speaker was an inspiration – brilliant.

> Great to have such a lively and enthusiastic keynote.

> The enthusiasm of the speaker was infectious. She has us in stitches a lot of the time!

3.1.3   Interactive Keynotes

Just as some lecturers may argue that a lecture hall does not lend itself to interaction, some keynote presenters may take a lead from the architecture and assume that the presentation should be a monologue. Just as we would challenge this idea in the case of lectures, we challenge it with regard to keynote addresses. No matter how interesting the speaker, attention can flag if participants are not actively involved. There are many ways that you can encourage your keynote speakers to include some form of interactivity. A few are included here.

3.1.3.1   *Activity*
The keynote engages the audience in debate by including short group discussion between two or three neighbours related to the conference theme.

3.1.3.2   *Voting*
Many lecture halls are now equipped with individual voting facilities which enable those in the auditorium to contribute views by voting on a small number of provided options. There are also a range of apps which can be used for this purpose. This actively is absorbing as the results are immediately available and can then be discussed. This can be used for serious purposes (for instance, anonymizing contribution regarding mental health) or more humorously (for instance, as an amusing ice-breaker).

An example of where this has been used very effectively is in an organization where a senior member of staff was due to speak about a specific change. While the change itself was not an issue, there were concerns about the timing and process. The voting opportunities gave those present an opportunity to voice those concerns anonymously and strongly. The speaker then addressed these issues at the start of her presentation. This then allowed those participating, having had the opportunity both to voice their concerns and hear them being acknowledged, to feel ready to listen to future plans and engage constructively.

3.1.3.3   *Answers and Questions*
We've already seen from the research, that respondents appreciate this opportunity. Ensure that the chair is able to handle this well by encouraging brisk questions from the floor and dealing with those that are too long, are self-serving of the questioner – or aren't actually a question!

3.1.3.4   *Emerging Keynotes*
Another possibility is for your speaker to deliver an emerging keynote. In this, the keynote will have already provided information on the conference website about their plans which will be highlighted to registrants who will have opportunities before the conference to ask questions, provide information and contribute views. The keynote can then use the lecture time to discuss the responses, taking into account the existing knowledge and interests of those present. The presentation is an evolving dialogue rather than a preset

monologue and acknowledges the audience and their views. Be aware, however, that this does take time to set up and organise and that your speaker must have time set aside well before their presentation to see the inputs to enable them to incorporate them in their address.

3.1.4 Keynotes – Practicalities

In Chapter 6 we talked about the desired virtues and abilities of your keynote – but where do you find this paragon? You and your colleagues will have knowledge of some of the key thinkers in the area and be aware of their work. But it is as important for one of you – or another colleague whose judgment you trust – to have seen the person speaking to an audience. As we all know from bitter experience, someone who is an excellent writer or researcher may not be a good keynote speaker.

Your keynote could be a respected person in your field but you may also want to cast your net wider. You could invite a student representative – perhaps the president of your institutional or national student association. Often such individuals with their recent experience as students and their fresh ideas and perspectives have a huge impact on an academic audience. As their role involves talking to different groups, they are likely to be fairly experienced speakers although audiences will relish an approach that is heartfelt and overlook any lack of polish if they do lack some experience. Offering this opportunity can enable your conference to have impact in other ways: in the UK, many national student associations' presidents go on to be our politicians and it will be warming to reflect that their oratory was honed at your event!

But just be aware that working with student representatives may be a little different from that with more conference-savvy keynote speakers and so may need you to spend more time making contact and being aware that there may be a different operating style.

3.1.4.1 *We Had This Experience*

We invited a national student leader to give a keynote at the end of the first day of a sector-wide conference and were delighted that he agreed – although it did involve a number of repeat emails before we eventually got a reply. We asked him to join us at the start of the conference but he didn't answer or arrive and as the time of his own presentation grew ever closer, we were getting a little worried. But 15 minutes before he was due to speak, our student keynote nonchalantly walked into the venue. When asked if he wanted help with his presentation or if he needed anything he said: 'No' and 'Please could I have a fried egg roll'. The very helpful catering staff obliged speedily and, duly fortified, he strolled into the plenary room, calmly inserted his USB stick into the computer, fixed his audience with an endearing smile and proceeded to give one of the most astute, insightful, and impassioned speeches about the student experience that we have ever had the privilege of hearing.

You should attempt to organise the keynote aspect of the conference programme early. Any good speaker is likely to have a full diary with commitments probably a long way off so it is essential to book them early on. This will also allow you to use their contribution as a selling point when you come to market your conference.

In inviting your keynote, you should provide as much information as you can about the conference. This will include details regarding their input: when you want them to speak, for how long, what time will be allocated to questions and answers etc. This is also the time to suggest interactivity if that is a preference. They will also need information about the theme and the evolving programme which will help them decide if they can contribute meaningfully and make a presentation which chimes with the ethos of the conference. They will also want to know about the delegates: how many will be there, are they a homogenous or diverse group, what is their existing knowledge of the area, will they be keen to interact etc.

This is also the time to discuss expenses and remuneration. It is appropriate to pay for all travelling expenses and overnight accommodation for the keynote so that they or their organisation is not out of pocket as a result of their contribution to your conference. Many conferences in the public sector do not routinely offer remuneration to keynotes who are already employed elsewhere. However, this is a difficult area to negotiate and in your invitation you could say tentatively:

> We will, of course, pay the expenses associated with your contribution to our conference including travel and subsistence together with costs of accommodation for the night before (or after) the keynote. Please also advise if there would be a fee.

Their response will then let you know what might be expected and if there is any opportunity for negotiation. Sometimes to get just THE right person a fee will be involved but their part in the conference will make that well worth it for both the impact they have on the event and the quantity of delegates that choose to register.

If you want the speaker to do more than give a keynote – perhaps to facilitate a workshop or to hand out awards at the end of the conference – this is the moment to ask them. After their contribution has been agreed, you should avoid the temptation of asking the keynote to do something beyond what you originally requested and to which they have committed.

Once the details are settled and confirmed, you should ask your keynote for a brief biography for use on the conference website. An early summary of what they propose to say is also very worthwhile as it will help you see how well their proposed talk resonates with the theme and content of your programme. At this stage, you can negotiate over this, for instance, by asking for emphasis in one area rather than another or for a specific allusion to be made to local issues or a new agenda. You may also advise further about the likely knowledge and experience of the audience if the summary suggests that the speaker has under- or over-estimated this. Once agreed, the summary should also be included on the conference website and in other marketing materials where it will be a draw to potential participants – while also helping them gain permission and funding to attend your conference. It surprises us just how many conferences do not ask their speakers for this or do not provide it to delegates as this is a selling point. In addition, prior information can mitigate against unfortunate misunderstandings which affect the contribution of keynotes and their impact at a conference.

Make sure that you keep in contact with your keynote as the planning process proceeds. They will be interested to know how the programme is shaping up and the interest that has been shown from potential participants. Some keynotes will appreciate much more: we were very impressed by an international speaker giving a keynote at a large sectoral conference in the UK who started his presentation by thanking the individual on the conference planning team who had spent much time on the phone to him answering questions and guiding him in the run up to the event.

Immediately before the conference, you will also want to obtain a copy of their presentation so that this can be loaded for them before they speak. There can be little worse for an unfortunate keynote than having 400 pairs of eyes on them as they fiddle unaided with an unfamiliar and uncooperative computer! You will also need to get masters for any handouts for participants if you decide to provide hard copies. Many organizers prefer to make the file available online either before or shortly after the conference.

On the big day, make sure the speaker is met at the venue, greeted and helped to meet any needs they have. In particular they will want to see the lecture hall before they speak, learn anything about the systems there they need to and see with their own eyes that their presentation is loaded. Inevitably, despite you having arranged for this beforehand, they are very likely to have 'tweaked' it the night before and be keen to use the new version! You should also ensure appropriate introductions are effected, in particular to the person who will be introducing them and/or chairing their sessions.

Ensure that the individual you have invited to introduce the opening keynote is definitely going to be able to stay for it. A warm introduction by a chair to the important, exciting talk ahead is marred if the person then explains that they can't stay for it as they have other important and exciting things to deal with... A very deflating start for speaker and participants alike! The speaker may also appreciate you passing on to the chair Grant's (2014) valuable advice on how not to introduce a speaker. Based on his speaking experience Grant describes how some introductions energise and excite while others do the opposite and impact negatively on the talk. He recommends chairs do not to read the speaker's biography, do not give away the speaker's content and do not try to make the speaker sound super-human as this can prove hard – and sometimes impossible – to live up to.

The chair introducing the speaker will also be responsible for organising the question and answer session which follows the presentation. As we saw from the research contributions in Section 1: Conference sessions: what do participants want?, our survey respondents were particularly clear on the dos and don'ts of questions and questioners, so pass on this advice to your chair. Also encourage them to think up a couple of questions of their own in case the participants have been stunned into silence by the talk! They should also thank the speaker – discussing briefly the impact their contribution has had and will have and encourage the participants to show their appreciation.

3.1.4.2 *What to Do When Things Go Wrong*

It is worth having a plan B ready in case the keynote is unable to attend at short notice. This happened to one of us, Celia. She says:

I happened to have a presentation prepared for another conference on a similar theme. Quickly putting the presentation onto the lecture hall system there was little time for nerves. This was completely serendipitous but as a result I now always have a plan for a discussion or activity on hand in case of disaster. Needless to say, now that I have a plan I have not been called on to use it.

Another problem can be the no-show of a speaker before the expected time of their keynote. This happened to one of us, Fiona. She says:

Once we realised that a transport issue had unavoidably delayed our initial keynote and they were not going to arrive in time, I quickly discussed a change of plan with the other speakers. Fortunately, the content of one to their talks was appropriate for earlier in the day and the speaker very kindly agreed to bring her keynote forward with very little notice. The speaker who had been detained then provided his contribution later in the day and, in the intervening time, had some opportunity to tweak it so it fitted better with the new placing in the conference programme. I was so very grateful for both their flexibility which, despite the problems, enabled the day to be seamless and valuable for those participating.

3.1.5 Alternative Conference Openings

In Chapter 7 we discussed inviting a keynote speaker. Here we look at some alternatives. A one-day conference is often book-ended by keynotes while a two or three-day event is likely to have a similar number of keynotes. There are many benefits to this. A keynote at the start of the second or third day of the conference can bring the same benefits as have been discussed for the opening keynote. They can inspire, engage, and set the tone for the day or days which follow. This is particularly valuable in conferences that have a daily registration option as delegates attending for only the second or third day of a conference will then have the same experience as from an opening keynote.

Closing the conference with a keynote is very worthwhile. It provides a last opportunity for delegates to come together for a final plenary – perhaps before a departing cup of tea. I always find this plenary an enjoyable way to end a conference with a bang: if delegates just leave after being divided up at parallel sessions, it can seem to end with a bit of a whimper. Another practical benefit of a closing keynote is that a big draw at the end of the conference to something engaging and relevant – or perhaps unusual or quirky – will keep your delegates there rather than starting their journeys home early.

3.1.6 Other Openings and Closings

We've discussed keynotes at length and they are indeed the time-honoured means of enabling a great conference experience. But you may also want to consider offering other openings or endings to your conference. What you choose will depend on your theme and the alternative experiences you want to create for your participants. The following could be used as well as or instead of a traditional keynote conference opening.

3.1.6.1 *Drama*

In a university conference focused on a particular approach to learning and teaching, students from their acting degree programme performed a ten-minute drama that showed what this might look like in practice. Participants found this an effective way to explain the detail which was conveyed clearly, succinctly, and humorously. They also particularly appreciated seeing the students' professional input which few staff had had the opportunity to witness before. The drama was later recorded and used for faculty development purposes.

3.1.6.2 *Student-Led Discussion*

In a sectoral conference focused on first year induction, students led a session describing their experiences and then initiated small group discussion with each student joining one group. The students' presence and their stories had an enormous impact on participants who also enjoyed their fresh and insightful contributions to the later discussions. Our research also showed that sessions with students added value when they were able to contribute their own perspectives and insights on the topics and issues under discussion.

3.1.7   'Work-in' or Maker Space

In an institutional conference focused on online learning, a giant 'work-in' was planned to give all participants the opportunity to engage with the new virtual learning environment. Much preparation was involved to devise a short but worthwhile hands-on introduction, to commandeer a large number of open-access computers and to ensure the availability of a good number of equipped people to support those needing help. The session was very popular and people left it pleased by the opportunity they had had to participate in a shared activity with colleagues across the institution and to gain practical and valuable knowledge which they could later build on.

Maker spaces are becoming increasingly popular where technology or equipment is made available for faculty and students who learn through experimenting. This can be incorporated in a conference either in plenary or as a parallel stream throughout the event. See the description of session types later in this chapter for more information.

4   Video Diaries

In a conference focused on the first-year student experience, video diaries were made by students acting the parts of different types of first year students: a school leaver, a mature student, an international student and so on. The recorded diary elements aimed to show their different experiences as they each reached the same points during the academic year: first week, first month, first semester etc. The students' scripts were created from genuine comments received in course evaluations. Participants were moved by hearing the students' voices knowing the words they were saying were authentic and by being made aware of some of the unexpected difficulties that first year students face navigating the transition into higher education. They also appreciated the humour in some of the scripts and the clever improvisations by the students acting the parts which made the diaries realistic.

5   Drama Again

In a professional association conference focused on student transitions, an educational drama company was commissioned to act out a short script which used student words recorded in interviews with transitioning students. The conference opened with the drama but it was not included in the programme and so provided a surprise start to the event which was enhanced by some of the actors being in the auditorium and contributing their character's voice from there. Participants were inspired by hearing the students' voices and their experiences and dilemmas. They also appreciated the opportunity for discussion during the drama when the action was 'frozen' for a short time.

> We saw and heard real stories which was very powerful.

> Seeing that dramatization of the feeling aspect, as well as the intellectual aspect of being at university – I thought that was very helpful.

Be mindful of the need for the drama to be presented professionally. While we have seen examples where this approach was used to good effect, we have also seen the opposite: a well-meant attempt at humour may backfire if it is overly amateur or perceived as being 'corny'. Cultural differences may have an impact. We have noted that British audiences tend to be more cynical than those in North America, for example.

6   Debate

A panel discussion or debate between two speakers can be used to great effect to stimulate discussion. Presenters may be chosen based on their known adherence to opposing views or approaches on a given subject. Alternatively, two people may elect to present an argument which may or may not align with their personal views.

These are just a few of the host of possible plenary sessions that you and your creative planning team could come up with to open your conference. Just be aware of the time that it can take to set up some of these interventions and the need for anonymity where real words are used.

Other possibilities specifically for conference closings are included below. As we said above when discussing closing keynotes, anything that brings a conference to a close should do so on a high so participants leave the event energised and enthusiastic.

7   Cabaret!

At a large international conference, a keynote of renown held an informal question and answer session – with all the 400 participants participating. The engaging and professional speaker had the rapt attention of the participants sitting in chairs (4 deep!) in a rough circle around him. Using a hand-held mic he ran the session like a successful cabaret act bringing in other session presenters, fielding questions and stimulating exchanges. Participants appreciated the opportunity to contribute and discuss issues in such an informal setting with such an eminent individual and were impressed by such a magnificent performance.

8   Résumé

At a large conference, an insightful and engaging speaker wrapped-up the event by summarizing the key messages. The presentation did require some organization with nominated people attending each of the sessions and feeding back to the speaker who could not be everywhere simultaneously. Participants found this to be a particularly useful session given the number of parallel sessions as it enabled them to learn something of the sessions they did not attend. They also appreciated how the speaker – who could think very quickly on his feet – was able to theme the conference outcomes very effectively and also highlight the celebratory aspects and recommend how they would translate into positive ways forward.

9   Awards

At an international conference, awards can be presented which focus on the conference: most original format, most valuable workshop, best poster. etc. Again, this requires some preparation as session evaluations have to be acquired and analyzed before the final plenary. An easier way to achieve this is to request nominations on paper before an advertised time. Alternatively, you could request online polling – although ensure this is achieved ethically. I once attended a conference when there was a huge number of votes for one presentation which turned out were coming from its presenter. At the ISATT (International Study Association on Teaching and Teachers), the delegates vote on presentations from prospective hosts for the next biennial conference.

At a professional association conference, the close is often used as a time to present the association's recognitions and awards. At an institutional conference, this time could be used for internal awards – such as learning, teaching and assessment best practice awards as voted for by students or a peer panel – or external awards such as professional recognition fellowships.

The presentation of awards is a surefire way of enthusing participants as it gives them a chance to consider their next steps in terms of achieving future awards themselves as well as giving them the opportunity to celebrate their colleagues' successes. Just be careful to build in enough time in case anyone decides to give a lengthy acceptance speech, or be ready to cut them off if necessary!

10   Parallel Sessions

Most conferences are likely to have a range of sessions that are run in parallel. These provide choice in the programme for participants and the opportunity for a large number of presenters and facilitators to share their work and research. Further information about these formats is provided in Chapter 4. The choice of format and organization will depend on the nature of your conference, with presentations such as research papers likely to dominate in research conferences and more interactive opportunities such as workshops dominating in developmental conferences.

Where possible, do encourage sessions to be proposed which include opportunities for activity, interactivity and sharing. As discussed in Chapter 7, we believe strongly that such sessions enable participants to do at conferences what they are there to do: to participate – and, as a result, they will learn more. So if you – and the peer review panel – want to see this in your conference, be explicit in the Call for Contributions and in the details requested of proposers in the Session Proposal Form.

10.1   *Parallel Sessions – Practicalities*

10.1.1   Shaping the Parallel Programme
Shape the programme by guiding proposers to the different session formats that you want to see at your conference. To achieve this:

– be explicit about format preferences in the *Call for Contributions*
– request these are clearly addressed in the *Session Proposal form*
– suggest certain types of sessions in the *Guidance* provided to presenters
– make these criteria in the selection of sessions on the *Peer Review* process
– provide an *award* for a particular session format or an innovative take on a format
– ensure *evaluation* questions include feedback on session formats and their impact.

Before we look at each of these below, do consider expectations for your conference. Most conferences held on an annual or biannual basis and linked to a professional organization or institution are likely to have built up over the years a certain way of running which has evolved gradually. Regular participants will have expectations in terms of formats and will be choosing to attend on this basis. Some of our survey respondents advised:

> Don't change the current format.

So to some extent, your decisions on sessions will be guided by the context in which your conference is being held. That is not to say innovations should not be considered – evolving approaches and formats are the lifeblood of conference sessions. But it is important to ensure the formats reflect the values of an organization and create an ethos which offers the experience which returning participants expect. It is important for your planning team to consider how to maintain the explicit and tacit characteristics of your organization's events. This should be facilitated if planning team members have experience of the conferences and there is participation in the group by a member of the planning team from the previous conference. If you are making significant changes to the nature or format of the conference sessions, you should make that clear to avoid any misunderstandings that could affect participants' enjoyment of the event and lose you repeat business.

11   Parallel Session Formats

We do not claim to offer an exhaustive list of all the potential sessions formats, instead what follows are some suggestions for formats that we have experienced. In each case we provide some guidance on the pros and cons of each in terms of their potential for engendering learning.

1   *Research paper* usually 30 or 45 minute presentation. The presenter writes a paper before the conference and then reads it in full, or precis, to the participants.

     Pros and cons for learning – this format is popular with researchers, especially those at an early stage in their career, because of the control provided to the speaker: the presentation is prepared in advance so little can go wrong. The problem is this is deathly dull and a waste of time. If the paper is written why not give it to the participants to read for themselves? It may be possible to advise presenters to use more engaging formats, such as highlighting insights from the work and engaging audience participation, or encouraging a pair of researchers to engage in a discussion with each other. Be aware, though, that this is a very popular format at many academic conferences, and changing behavior can be challenging. Make it very clear in the conference details that proposals are more likely to succeed if they build in interaction than if a paper is read, if this is the case.

What the organizer needs to provide – possibly nothing, but usually a computer and projector in case the presenter wishes to project the paper or key points from it as they read it.

2 *Interactive workshop*. The nature of the workshop will vary enormously, but the key characteristic is the focus on what the participants, not just the presenter, are doing. Many conferences require proposals to include timings of activities to ensure true interaction will occur.

Pros and cons for learning – as we have discussed earlier, learning is more likely to occur when participants are engaged. However, there can be a danger with having completely content free sessions. Some balance is required.

What the organizer needs to provide – typically the organizer provides a room that has flexible seating, a computer and a projector. Presenters may be expected to bring any other props that they require, but some organizers provide flipcharts, plenty of colored pens and sticky notes as standard kit in the presentation room.

3 *Maker space*. This is an opportunity for participants to try out something for themselves. Typically, this involves some sort of software or technology, for example 3D printers, video editing programmes, lecture response systems, virtual learning environments. The premise is that participants have the opportunity to play with a resource, and create something for themselves, within a short space of time. The intent is not to give the participant the expertise they will need to use the resource, but to give them an idea of how the resource can be used and some confidence in using it in the future.

Pros and cons for learning – this can be a highly interactive session popular with participants. The disadvantage is the time needed to prepare for and support a successful maker space.

What the organizer needs to provide – depending on the resources that are included this can be quite time consuming. Ideally prepare handouts that guide the participant to create something tangible using the resource that can be completed within 10 to 15 minutes. If the resources are computer based provide sufficient laptops or tablets, ensure the software is installed and available. Volunteers should be on hand to assist as needed and to provide security for the equipment.

4 *Round Table/Cracker Barrel*. This is a plenary event set out in café style. Each presenter sits at a table with up to 10 participants. Timing is such that participants can attend two or three tables within the session.

Pros and cons for learning – this gives an opportunity for participants to hear about a number of topics within a short space of time. While time is limited this may allow for more in-depth conversation with the presenter than is the case with the more traditional presentation, but it can also mean that the topic can only be addressed on a superficial level.

What the organizer needs to provide – a room set out with tables and chairs for 10 to 12. Timing is important so someone must take control and end each round table session promptly to ensure the full cycle is completed.

5 *Recorded presentation/Silent session.* This is particularly useful in a conference where a presenter is unable to attend in person. The presentation is recorded in advance and projected into the conference, either as a plenary or a break out session.

Pros and cons for learning – participants are able to hear from a presenter who would not otherwise be able to attend, but there may be limited opportunities for interaction. Improving internet connections make it easier to attend live from a distance through a conferencing system than used to be the case. If this is possible then the presenter is able to answer questions from the participants, but is not strictly 'silent'!

What the organizer needs to provide – a computer and projector to display the presentation, if using conference software then a reliable internet connection is also required.

6 *Un-conference or Connection Café.* An example of this was provided at a conference included in our research (see Introduction).

Pros and cons for learning – the onus is on the participants to decide what they want to hear about or to discuss. As with active learning, the participants control the process and are therefore more likely to be actively engaged in the process. If the group of participants is particularly diverse then this may not be a productive use of time, as the number of topics may lead to very small groups.

What the organizer needs to provide – space in the programme to allow for the collection of nominated topics, rooms with appropriate furniture to host the event and someone to keep time.

7 *World Café.* Tables are set out with blank flipchart paper or white paper table cloths. Participants are asked to address an aspect of a particular topic. The discussion is recorded on the flipchart or table cloth. After a set amount of time they move to another table, possibly leaving one member of the group at the original table to provide context. Once at the new table they are asked to read the comments made by the previous group and then address the same topic from another perspective. This may be repeated 4 to 6 times. Depending on numbers and organization the group may end up

back at their original table where they can review the comments made in their absence.

Pros and cons for learning – this can be a highly effective method to focus discussion on a key topic, particularly one that involves multiple perspectives or aspects. It should not be used where a free-flowing open discussion is anticipated as the structure may prove inhibiting for participants.

What the organizer needs to provide – a suitable room with tables and chairs in café style, flip chart paper or paper table clothes, pens. It is vital that timings are worked out in advance and strictly observed. An alternative to this involves using dialogue sheets

11.1   *Dialogue Sheets*

A Dialogue Sheet is a simple but powerful physical tool which stimulates effective and democratic professional conversation by structuring discussion, encouraging contributions and recording outcomes. Dialogue Sheet methodology was developed for change management purposes from the World Café as described above. Tables are set out each with the same pre-printed Dialogue Sheet (usually A1 or A2 size) addressing a particular issue. Participants at each table take turns at reading the questions posed, discussing views and logging the outcomes on the sheet.

Pros and cons for learning – Dialogue Sheets provide a neutral targeted space for dialogue to be logged which encourages the airing of opinions and the sharing of views and empower all taking part by democratizing discussion with all views welcomed and respected. They are effective in encouraging participation and engagement while the opportunity to log the discussion on the sheet ensures the outcomes are recorded for later analysis. Preparing Dialogue Sheets does take time to ensure the discussions stimuli are appropriate for the context and the participants and, importantly, are attractive and enjoyable to use. There is an on-cost involved in designing and replicating a resource of this size.

8 *Panel presentation.* Three to five presentations are made in the same time slot. These are usually grouped thematically.

Pros and cons for learning – panels are an effective way of managing several presentations within one slot, and if grouped thematically are useful for participants interested in that particular theme. A disadvantage may arise if the organizers' interpretation of a theme does not agree with that of the participants, in which case the participant may feel obligated to sit through three or four irrelevant presentations in order to hear the one they are interested in.

What the organizer needs to provide – rooms and equipment as for any presentation and a time keeper to ensure presenters end on time, and if necessary, to facilitate a question and answer session at the end.

9   *Student and faculty presentation.* While students are often welcome to present at conferences, they may be reluctant to do so through a lack of confidence that their work has yet reached a stage where it can be shared. This is unfortunate, as not only does the student miss out on an opportunity to build their confidence and gain experience, but the academic community loses a chance to hear about breakthrough work. One way to address this is to encourage faculty and students to co-present. The presentation may be led by either student or faculty or be truly joint.

Pros and cons for learning – the inclusion of student and faculty joint presentations in the proposal sets the tone for a conference, indicating that both are equally welcome and valued.

What the organizer needs to provide – the same requirements as for any session. Additional support in preparation and presentation may be needed for the student presenters if they are inexperienced.

10 *Walk and Talk.* Take the presentation out of the classroom and make use of the location. At an international conference in Edinburgh, for instance, one of us, Fiona, co-led a session which involved discussing approaches with a partner while visiting some of the scenic sites close to the venue. She says:

Many participants noted that the session made a welcome change from their usual conference experience where they saw little of the city where they were staying. The session concluded with a group discussion on our return where Tweets and photos sent during the walk were viewed and the benefits of talking, walking – and doing both together! were shared. In another example at a conference held in Edge Hill in 2017, participants were led on a 'Twalk'. They walked in small groups around a predetermined route, tweeting responses to set questions at 5 minute intervals. The organizers shared this with colleagues unable to attend the conference, with the result that people were able to participate in their own walks on campuses around the world.

Pros and cons for learning – a change of location can be highly effective in stimulating new thoughts and freeing one from habitual thought processes. It is also good for our health as it counters the common experience of conference goers who seem to spend more time eating and less time exercising than they do at home.

What the organizer needs to provide – someone to be at a base and someone to participate in the walk. Time is also needed to plan and recce. the route, consider alternative places in the event of bad weather on the day, arrange partnering and to prepare the activities.

11 *Pecha Kucha* – This quick-fire presentation style uses a format that was first introduced in 2003. Presenters prepare 20 images each of which is visible for 20 seconds, while the presenter talks. See http://www.pechakucha.org/ for more information and guidance.

Pros and cons for learning – this format ensures that presentations are one time, as the slides advance automatically. As with other quick fire approaches the benefits are that the presenter keeps to topic and several presentations can be covered in a relatively short time. At the same time, they can be overly superficial given the restrictions imposed by the format.

What the organizer needs to provide – as with other presentations, a computer and projector is usually all that is needed. A timekeeper, although optional, is helpful, as although the timing of the presentation is automatic, participants may well have questions or wish to engage in a discussion which will need to be facilitated.

13 Networking Opportunities: How to Enable Learning

For the many good reasons discussed in Chapters 1 and 2, networking opportunities should be explicit within a conference programme with many and varied occasions provided. Effective networking can range from a simple but successful strategy – such as just providing coffee, a large space and plenty of time in the programme – to more formal opportunities which push participants into networking with those that they don't know. As some people don't have the confidence or natural skills to initiate networking, formal networking enables them to benefit from all that professional engagements with others can bring. We'll now consider:

– Informal networking
– Formal networking

13.1 *Informal Networking*
This can take many forms and a few suggestions are provided below:

13.1.1 Provide a Delegate List
One of the most useful tools for networking is the Delegate List, which should always be provided in conference packs.

13.1.2 Create Specific Locations
This can just involve a place where people feel comfortable together with some refreshments.

Good opportunities to strike up conversation between participants – liked the networking area with the coffee, juice etc. Made it a convivial and productive place to hang out!

13.1.3   Employ Existing Space in the Programme
Encourage networking by labelling certain spaces in the programme as networking opportunities.

I learned a lot from informal networking in the coffee break and at lunch.

13.1.4   Create Specific Times
Designate certain times as specifically for networking. Here are some examples.

13.1.5   New Participants' Breakfast
Those new to your conference may feel a little outside the social aspect of it particularly if many of those attending are already known to each other and there are many ways you can break the ice for them to enable them to get the most out of the conference. A very valuable way is to include a specific time – such as a breakfast – where they can meet members of the conference planning group, conference committee or professional association chairs and, importantly, other new delegates. This enables them to begin networking early and they can then build on the contacts they have made later in the conference.

13.1.6   Conference Dinner
Social occasions such as the conference dinner provide excellent opportunities for meeting others and beginning to network. Help with this by finding ways to encourage participants to sit at a table with people they do not know. They will often be surprised at the welcome they receive and the connections they make. Also find ways to help participants mingle more: could people be encouraged to move to another table with their after-dinner coffee, chat over a drink in the bar, be tempted onto the dance floor?

The difficulty with arranging networking, however, is getting the balance right between being heavy-handed about it or providing too light a touch.

We once organized a conference and were pleased with the amount of networking time we had created within the programme. There were specific networking sessions included and then in all the breaks we encouraged people to network by saying this explicitly in the programme:

'Networking with coffee'

'Lunch and networking'

'Network at the evening reception'

We received some useful feedback which said:

> OK we've got it. There is the chance to network at every opportunity. But you don't have to say it every time!

13.2   *Formal Networking*

Formal networking involves some form of deliberate interactivity that brings people together. This can be a very useful way of including new conference participants, promoting active networking early in the conference and avoiding the kind of unconscious cliqueiness which can arise when many participants are already well known to each other. There are a host of group ice-breaker activities you could consider for your conference. A few of the possibilities which are suitable for formal networking follow. All of them require a space and time slot designated for the activity within the programme.

13.2.1   Meeting by Numbers – or Colours

This is a very simple device for encouraging networking. Firstly, pre-arrange for your participants' badges to include a number or coloured dot. Then, invite participants in the session to speak about themselves or an aspect of the conference theme to others with the same number or colour. This could result in several discussions taking place between people not previously known to each other which can reap benefits during the conference. This could just be a familiar face to hook up with later or it could lead to a sharing of experiences and aspirations, a discussion centred on ideas and views – and, potentially, collaborative rewards beyond.

13.2.2   'Speed Dating'

This device requires a little more organizing. First participants are paired. Each individual within each pair then discusses a particular theme or interest of theirs for five minutes with their partner. A bell advises they should switch roles and discuss the interests of the other individual for another five minutes. Another bell advises that each individual should pair up with someone else – again pre-arranged to continue their discussion. There is no need to match people with similar experiences or interests etc. The very randomness of the pairings can bring its own successful results.

Despite the artificiality of the set-up, the very formality of the arrangement and the fixed times for exchanges, enables this to be a surprisingly fertile opportunity to solidify ideas and plans through the act of sharing and to gain valuable and spontaneous feedback. We have found it very useful for sharing our interests and gaining valuable feedback on them and learning about and contributing to input from others. Surprisingly, that includes colleagues with whom we already work closely and so the format itself seems to unleash fresh and generous insights.

> And now...
>
> ...its 4pm on the final day of the conference. Your conference is over. Most of the participants have now left amid enthusiastic goodbyes to those they have met, learned from or with whom they have shared experiences – and perhaps a bottle of wine. Others remain and are still in small groups deep in conversation about potential new links, collaborations and research together with plans for innovations and changes they intend to implement when they return to their institution. All of this has resulted from the learning that has been achieved in the sessions and networking opportunities you offered within the conference programme. Result! Well done!

References

Grant, A. (2014). How not to introduce a speaker. *Huffington Post.* Retrieved from http://www.huffingtonpost.com/adam-grant/how-not-to-introduce-a-sp_b_5073251.html

Simmons, N. (2010). *Renewing my scholarship: Journeys away* (Centre for Teaching Excellence Blog). Waterloo: University of Waterloo. Retrieved from http://ctge-blog.uwaterloo.ca/?p=1490

Beyond the Individual: Planning for Impact at the Institutional, Regional and National Level

Erika Kustra, Jessica Raffoul and Beverley Hamilton

Where is the beginning, where is the end of an event? The "social drama" (Turner, 1975) of an academic gathering has its pre-text, that is, it bases itself and relies on the practices preparing it. The event actually begins long before it officially does. It takes its wayward beginning with many veiled and secret stories.
> FRIESE (2001)

Conferences are a vehicle for the dissemination and exchange of new ideas or knowledge. However, presenters and organizers often hope that the ideas or practices explored at conferences will do more than just circulate: that they will move outward and onward from the event itself, optimizing conference outcomes to include sustained change at the institutional, regional, or national level. To date there has been little research regarding the effectiveness of conferences in fostering sustained change – either in perspectives or in action.

This chapter will explore one university's evolving efforts to use conferences to identify, explore, and strengthen institutional and provincial change initiatives, pinpointing and promoting specific intended outcomes at numerous levels. Through the planning of more than a dozen regional,

© KONINKLIJKE BRILL NV, LEIDEN, 2018 | DOI 10.1163/9789004373013_009

national, and international conferences, we have found that the process of conceptualizing and organizing the conference – the strategic engagement of multiple communities, the structural choices, the careful situation of the event in the context of other opportunities and network development plans – significantly enhances the potential for conferences to have lasting impact. In developing this approach, we have drawn on research exploring the functions of conferences in academics' lives and disciplinary work, and the implications of the distributed nature of post-secondary leadership in change initiatives.

1   Revisiting the Event – And Its Context

Gross and Fleming (2011) undertook case studies of faculty members' experiences of academic conferences and of the impact of those experiences on knowledge making. They focused in particular on the purpose of conferences in new and emerging fields of research, and on the role of conferences in assisting academics to cross boundaries into cognate or evolving fields of research. They identified the following key functions:

– establishing, excavating, or reinforcing common values;
– establishing or strengthening aspirational communities;
– developing, legitimizing, or questioning normative knowledge structures;
– defining bodies of knowledge as worthy of study, and legitimizing deviations from traditional norms in epistemology; and
– establishing or reinforcing collective identities within emerging disciplinary fields.

These functions seem to be particularly salient in exploring and articulating the goals and challenges involved in supporting and extending the scholarship of teaching and learning in post-secondary settings, for example. Across many disciplines, scholars continue to struggle to legitimize, to find allies in, and to establish increasingly significant networks in eliciting funding for such research. We host a joint annual conference, focused on the systematic study of teaching and learning, with another institution. While such research is relatively conventional within centres for teaching and learning, pursuing and legitimizing this research across disciplines remains, for many, a field of contested legitimacy (e.g., Boshier, 2009). This international annual conference has been a key lever in moving this work forward at our institutions.

    When we launched this effort over ten years ago, our objective was to enable instructors at our two institutions to share their experiences researching teaching and learning, and for them to interact with others who were similarly engaged in such scholarship. Scholars often become intrigued with the scholarship of their disciplines idiosyncratically. The conference offered an important bridge to engage with the pedagogical discourse in their fields, and over the years, as attendance nearly tripled, it became clear that through our efforts we were building awareness of critical issues in teaching and learning and offering valued opportunities for engagement. However, at the end of the event, when faculty returned to their disciplinary silos, we struggled to sustain momentum, and many of the critical, timely initiatives lost traction.

We developed a better understanding of levers to address this challenge through an exploration of the ways in which change occurs in universities and colleges. Very little has been written about educational leadership in Canadian post-secondary contexts (Wright et al., 2014b). However, extensive European and Australian research suggests that "distributed" leadership, which disperses the powers and responsibilities of leadership among multiple individuals, and among groups at multiple levels of the university (see Bolden et al., 2009; Roxå & Mårtensson, 2013; Southwell & Morgan, 2009), is most typical, and when strategically leveraged, most effective.

The distributed leadership model reflects the ways that hierarchies and knowledge networks interact in academic settings. Members of a university work through social and information networks to navigate and make meaning across the system. Over time, emergent leaders develop within these significant networks, whether or not they occupy a role of formal authority. Because of the powerful influence of these significant networks, distributed leadership can be an effective way to bring about change in complex adaptive systems like universities (Hamilton & Graniero, 2012): however, these leaders operate most effectively in a context of constructive collaboration with the formal leadership of their institutions. Sterman (2006) describes the ways in which people understand, interpret, react to, and evade imposed measures in systems similar to universities, resulting in highly unpredictable and often counterintuitive outcomes: these networks are critical to the impact of interventions and initiatives. Coordination of "top-down" and "bottom-up" perspectives and activities is a central challenge of institutional leadership (Bolden et al., 2009). Given these complexities, it is little wonder that effecting systemic and sustainable change in post-secondary institutions can be "slippery". Repeated engagement with multiple networks, and acknowledging those networks' concerns and narratives, can provide some traction, if such engagement is flexible and measured enough to account for the ways in which networks operate (Hamilton & Raffoul, 2016; Mowles, 2011).

Given this understanding of the post-secondary context, and Gross and Fleming's (2011) identified functions of an academic conference, the conference itself – the one to three-day event – is one step in the larger process of planning for change. In other words, conferences can be a critical lever in effecting change, but not an automatic one. The conference cannot be viewed in isolation: it is part of a larger process that takes into account the organization and planning process, events that precede or follow from it, the networks of people involved during planning and implementation, the exercise of peer review, the financial outcomes, and how the event is situated within an institution (Becker & Clark, 2001). Understood as a process, conferences and their organizers can intervene at multiple points in the post-secondary system, energizing varied networks, and offering academics, students, and staff opportunities to reinforce or reconfigure their institutional identities.

2   Conference Planning Phase

2.1   *Identifying Key Players*
Ideally, conference organization should begin one to two years in advance with the appointment of key players and committee structures. It's important to intentionally plan for engagement of stakeholders at multiple levels and in all roles, considering both the impact you hope to achieve, and the level at which you hope to do so. If change is intended at the institutional level, involve formal leaders like Department Heads, Deans, and upper administrators as well as informal leaders like faculty, staff, and students. If you intend to plan for change at the regional or national level, consider integrating members from other institutions in the area or from government bodies. This involvement can take many forms including:

- co-sponsoring/co-hosting the event or a feature of the event;
- participation as members of one of the conference planning committees, steering committee, or review board;
- providing feedback on the design of the conference, or choice of theme and keynote speakers;
- filling specific roles during the conference such as panel chairs, session judges, session co-facilitators;
- presenting at the event;
- providing financial support; and
- participation in grant applications to fund the event.

As a border institution, we partner with an American university to host our annual teaching and learning conference. Funded in part by the Provosts of both universities, this cross-border collaboration alternates between the two campuses annually, and has proved an excellent opportunity for academics and graduate students to present and to become exposed to discipline-based, international teaching and learning research and issues in a local environment. It has helped to foster new relationships internationally and across additional institutions in Canada. The Conference has led to further partnerships, for example, on a recently successful Social Sciences and Humanities Research Council Connections Grant to fund the upcoming conference. This partnership has enabled us to more easily identify current and emerging issues in teaching and learning intended to impact institutional and government policies.

2.2   *Selecting a Theme and Early Promotion*

The selection of a theme can increase the potential influence of a conference. Research new and emerging institutional and/or governmental high-impact projects and policies. What are people concerned with? Where is the money coming from and where is it going? If selected carefully, a theme can attract attention and galvanize involvement of people beyond those traditionally involved in the conference. For example, teaching evaluation is a contentious area with increasing focus for stakeholders, provincial governments, institutions, and instructors (Jones, 2014). In 2014, we were part of a multi-institutional team that undertook a provincially funded feasibility study exploring the potential of establishing a core teaching evaluation approach for the Province of Ontario (Wright et al., 2014a). Despite the fact that there have been more than 17,000 studies published on teaching evaluation, the pathway towards truly effective teaching evaluation at post-secondary institutions, which is critical to ongoing pedagogical improvement, has been "slippery" at best (Hénard & Roseveare, 2012; Raffoul & Hamilton, 2016). As one element of an ongoing effort to improve our practices institutionally, and also to create greater synergy across institutions, we focused a portion of one year's conference on teaching evaluation, inviting teams from across Canada and Michigan to come and explore possible change initiatives that they can then bring back to their institutions and use to inform policy.

It might also help to choose a theme with a bit of an edge – pushing the limits of a change initiative – but still familiar enough that participants can contribute. For example, in 2013, the Ontario Minister of Training, Colleges, and Universities noted that higher education is in a period of "revolution, not evolution". And "innovate or die" was a recurring theme at a summit co-sponsored by the Carnegie Corporation and the Bill and Melinda Gates Foundation on the Future of Higher Education. Building off of this momentum, we chose to focus our conference on the theme, "On the Verge: Debating the Future of Higher Education", and began advertising the event with a single, edgy image by email, on postcards distributed at national and international events, and a web landing page.

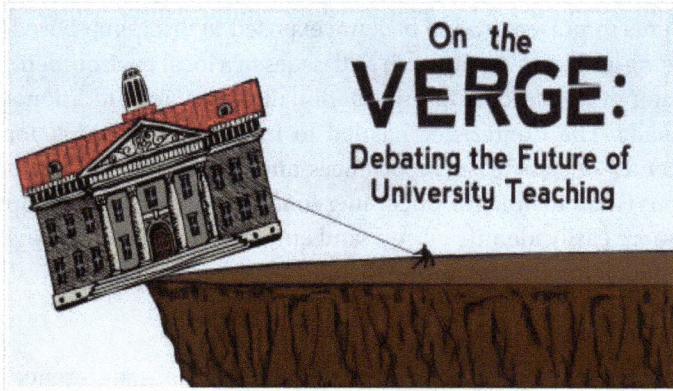

2.3   *Professional Development Opportunities*

Provide opportunities to raise awareness of and facility with the conference theme. This can help maximize attendance and encourage those who would not normally submit proposals feel more comfortable contributing, and possibly find new ways to effect change and impact initiatives in their home institutions. Leading up to our annual conference, we have facilitated campus-wide workshops focused on the conference theme roughly one month prior to the conference proposal submission deadline. During these interactive sessions, faculty, staff, and students are able to brainstorm possible proposal topics and possibly partner with others interested in similar areas of focus. We have also hosted weekly, informal, lunch-time book clubs: in 2015, Geoff Scott, international expert in the area of educational leadership, was to deliver the opening plenary at our teaching and learning conference focused on leadership, so ramping up to the event, we read and discussed his seminal book, *Turnaround Leadership for Higher Education* during a lunch-time book club. Participants were better prepared to engage with Scott, participate in the sessions, and develop partnerships with others interested in the same area of focus. One of our more effective initiatives has been tying small or large grants to the theme of the conference, both before and after the event. This encourages reflection on the topic, extends the inquiry inspired by the conference, facilitates the development of cross-disciplinary projects, and enables groups to engage in projects over a period of time, leading initiatives in a distributed fashion (Morris & Fry, 2006; Nimmo & Littlejohn, 2009). The conference can then serve as a way of sharing the outcomes from the projects with a larger audience. The impact of the grants can be increased by offering higher funding options for grant proposals that come from collaborations across department or across institutions.

The key takeaway here is that you should provide opportunities centred around and designed to help fuel interest in and facility with the conference theme, resulting in a higher chance for cross-campus engagement. When a theme can be tied to a number of initiatives and activities within an institution, and even nationally, and that occur intentionally over a period of a year or more, the impact of the conference itself can be maximized and extended.

2.4   Conference Structure

The structure of the conference can influence its potential impact. A common model includes an invited keynote presenting to all participants, followed by breakout groups with peer-reviewed sessions and a peer-reviewed poster session.

There are however alternative formats that may serve different purposes (see Chapter 8). For example, a consensus conference is focused around a citizens' panel – a collection of lay people who are given the task of deliberating policy issues in order to improve decision making for policies (Guston, 1999). In this model, a steering committee provides the organizing structure, and staff provide support, while the lay people deliberate like a jury, and experts provide advice to aid in the deliberation. The goal for this form of conference is a change in policy, a change in public understanding, as well as the change in expert understanding in the context of the lay discussions. A review of the first use of this model in the US indicated significant learning as result of the interaction between experts and non-experts, and they suggested that greater impact would likely result with more opportunities for informal interchange (Guston, 1999).

Another format is a symposium intentionally designed to inform public policy. Experts are invited to present, and a small group chosen by the conference delegates draft a document describing the agreement position reached by those at the symposium (Aubrey et al., 2002).

Conferences can also be structured around intended concrete outcomes. This might include, for example, group activities designed to create a preliminary outline for a chapter or article, which would then be drafted and revised after the conference. Another approach sees institutional teams preparing a project plan, with integrated keynotes, concurrent sessions, and facilitated work periods. In some cases this may also involve assignments or activities leading into the event.

2.5   Experts and Guest Speakers

Select a keynote speaker and/or other expert speakers and facilitators with the aim of increasing the sphere of influence. Consider bringing in national or international participants depending on their reputation, or attracting the attention of academic administrators who might not normally participate. The expert from 'away' is often seen as more convincing even if the same message is shared. For example, at our conference focused on the future of higher education, we hosted a pre-conference forum, and invited provosts, vice-provosts teaching and learning, deans, faculty, and students from across the country to debate the positive and negative view of the future of post-secondary education. This attracted a broader audience than would have been typical for a teaching and learning event on our campus.

In some cases, it can also be critical to include faculty members and students as speakers. They can speak to academic experience on the ground framing the challenges, needs, and response to issues realistically, critically, and persuasively. Divergent voices – people from the community with varied views and perspectives – enrich our understanding. They also establish a context where open dialogue is clearly encouraged. A range of speakers, with different roles and with different networks, can have a strong influence both on who comes to an event and how they react to the ideas presented.

3   Conference Implementation Phase

Part of the goal of the conference is to involve and share information, joint vocabulary, and develop increased awareness. Some events can be developed either just prior to the conference, or during the conference that can increase the involvement and integration of people likely to contribute to change.

3.1   *Pre-Conference Workshop, Forum, or Meetings*
Workshops or meetings with the keynote or selected speakers with institutional stakeholders can be a powerful opportunity to bring together Heads, Associate Deans, Deans and other upper administrators to discuss issues of importance to them, in the context of the external expert.

At many events, we invite experienced faculty members to act as table hosts for breakout and group discussions. This mediates the process of getting discussions started. Table hosts, who usually have an interest in the topic and who have often participated in many of the activities leading up to the conference, also act as sources of information. They can smooth over challenging table dynamics, and in the case of a controversial conference focus, table hosts can act as liaisons for organizers, signalling in case difficult situations arise.

3.2   *Networking*
As discussed in Chapter 1, networking is a critical part of conferences. Often conferences attract people with a specific focus or discipline. If the goal of

the conference is larger scale impact, intentionally inviting stakeholders and key players from other spheres and providing networking opportunities can increase the reach of your event. This may involve thoughtful design of interactive sessions, or the extension of informal networking and meeting times. The key element here is ensuring that people who do not normally have an opportunity to interact have a chance to develop connections and a common set of experiences and vocabulary. It is important to keep in mind that participants often make their key discoveries talking with others over coffee breaks. Optional networking lunches, easily organized by inviting possible themes and then posting signs on those themes at various lunch tables, can be very useful extensions of those informal networking opportunities.

Change in behaviour that continues past the conference itself is more likely to occur with extended contact, based on the rationale and evidence that extended professional development opportunities are more likely to result in changes in behaviour than short interventions (Gibbs & Coffey, 2004). For example, the *Inquiry Experience* is a networking plan where participants can choose to join a group with common interests. They are put in contact prior to the conference, and meet with a facilitator each day throughout the conference. The facilitator helps the group to identify common interests or desired outcomes. The group uses the conference as a way to gain information, and then integrate their learning together. After the event, groups can write and publish a paper, develop an action group, plan for additional meetings, and so on. Variations of this model have been integrated into specific conferences such as the 2002 Society for Teaching and Learning in Higher Education (STLHE), *Fostering the Spirit of Inquiry* at McMaster University, and the 2016 Educational Developers Caucus (EDC) Educational Developers Without Borders.

Another model for networking and extended interaction is the development of Action Groups or Writing Retreats both of which involve clear, identified outcomes. Examples are the Educational Developers Caucus Action Groups that meet throughout the year, prepare a report for the annual conference, and often use the annual conference as an opportunity for face-to-face meetings (https://www.stlhe.ca/affiliated-groups/educational-developers-caucus/edc-special-projects-action-groups/).

4   Post-Conference Phase

One of the key elements of extending impact beyond the individual is to intentionally consider how the work of the conference will continue after the event formally ends.

4.1   *Sharing Narratives: Resources and Research after the Conference*

Consider how the information from the conference will be reported following the conference. Many societies require a report from the hosts, but this report often has a small sphere of readers. Alternatively, sharing slides, handouts, and resources from the conference can act as a repository. The Professional and Organizational Development Network (POD) has been highly effective in sharing resources for several years, using an electronic platform (http://podnetwork.org/wikipodia/). The conference website can also function as a record of the event: make sure the website is fully up to date if you intend to leave it up. Pictures, Twitter archives, reports, and other materials can be stored on the site for others' future use or review. Finally, online discussion boards focused on the conference themes may provide an opportunity for participants to continue the conversation.

Another way of capturing the resources and extending the impact following the conference is through publications. Many conferences have proceedings, and some have associated journals such as the STLHE journal *Collected Essays of Learning and Teaching* (CELT) that publishes peer-reviewed articles based on sessions offered at the conference. An alternative approach is to create a book that focuses on core themes of the conference, with a more intentionally and proactively selective approach to authors and topics. This provides the opportunity for a more focused and thematically integrated publication than is typical of proceedings. Taking this approach requires considerable forethought, if the book and the conference are to be developed in parallel. Those involved have to find a publisher early, to ensure that the themes, development, and shape of the book will fit with a publishing house's mandate and standards.

Some institutions consistently encourage participants to share what they learned from the conference with colleagues who were unable to attend, either through lunch meetings, presentations or workshops. For example, a quote from a participant,

> After the conference, we contributed our own session to university staff and this has been developed into internal training.

This process encourages participants to integrate ideas from conferences into the needs and culture of their home institutions, which can provide a helpful mediating step in moving towards extended engagement. Presenting can also cement a sense of ownership or connection with new ideas, and attract other interested people to create critical mass for an idea.

Some conference organizers build the action planning right into the conference. At an interactive closing plenary, for example, participants at one of our conferences committed to something – practical and deliberate – that they intended to do in the next year, which they wrote on a card and which acted as a "reminder to self". A further step in helping people keep their resolutions is to ask them to write their plan on a postcard which is then mailed to them as a "reminder to self" a few weeks after the conference.

5   Conclusion

If the sole aim of conferences was the dissemination of knowledge, numerous less costly, less troublesome, and more efficient activities could achieve that goal. Conferences have intellectual, social, political, and affective dimensions. They create spaces for collective exploration, for identity formation, for the development of communities and value systems, for the legitimation of new ways of doing things, and for the questioning of orthodoxies. The narratives generated and shared at conferences have the potential to help move relevant initiatives and cultural change forward, but this result is not an automatic outcome of hosting a conference. In a process of change, a conference can be a crystallizing moment: one that enables the articulation of new ideas, but also that also encourages stocktaking and reflection with like-minded people. Fullan and Scott (2009) argue that change is collective learning: a conference – from initial planning through to final reporting – provides many opportunities to foster learning. Intentional planning for those opportunities is a key to impact.

References

Aubry, M., Cantu, R., Dvorak, J., Graf-Baumann, T., Johnston, K., Kelly, J., Lovell, M., McCrory, P., Meeuwisse, W., & Schamasch, P. (2002). Summary and agreement statement of the First International Conference on Concussion in Sport, Vienna 2001. *British Journal of Sports Medicine, 36*(1), 6–7.

Becker, P., & Clark, W. (Eds.). (2001). *Little tools of knowledge: Historical essays on academic and bureaucratic practices.* Ann Arbor, MI: The University of Michigan Press.

Bolden, R., Petrov, G., & Gosling, J. (2009). Distributed leadership in higher education: Rhetoric and reality. *Educational Management Association and Leadership, 37*(20), 257–277.

Boshier, R. (2009). Why is the scholarship of teaching and learning such a hard sell? *Higher Education Research and Development, 28*(1), 1–15.

Friese, H. (2001). Thresholds in the ambit of discourse: On the establishment of authority at academic conferences. In P. Becker & W. Clark (Eds.), *Little tools of knowledge: Historical essays on academic and bureaucratic practices* (pp. 285–310). Ann Arbor, MI: The University of Michigan Press.

Fullan, M., & Scott, G. (2009). *Turnaround leadership for higher education.* San Francisco, CA: Jossey-Bass.

Gibbs, G., & Coffey, M. (2004). The impact of training of university teachers on their teaching skills, their approach to teaching and the approach to learning of their students. *Active Learning in Higher Education, 5*(1), 87–100.

Gross, N., & Fleming, C. (2011). Academic conferences and the making of philosophical knowledge. In C. Camic, N. Gross, & M. Lamont (Eds.), *Social knowledge in the making* (pp. 151–179). Chicago, IL: The University of Chicago Press.

Guston, D. H. (1999). Evaluating the first US consensus conference: The impact of the citizens' panel on telecommunications and the future of democracy. *Science, Technology, & Human Values, 24*(4), 451–482.

Hamilton, B., & Graniero, P. (2012). Disruptive cartography in academic development. *International Journal of Academic Development, 17*(3), 243–258.

Hamilton, B., & Raffoul, J. (2016, June). *Made to slip: Why good initiatives lose traction.* Paper presented at the Annual Conference of the Society for Teaching and Learning in Higher Education, London.

Hénard, F., & Roseveare, D. (2012). *Fostering quality teaching in higher education: Policies and practices.* An Institutional Management in Higher Education (IMHE) guide for higher education institutions. Retrieved from http://www.oecd.org/edu/imhe/QT%20policies%20and%20practices.pdf

Jones, G. A. (2014). An introduction to higher education in Canada. In K. M. Joshi & S. Paivandi (Eds.), *Higher education across nations* (pp. 1–38). New Delhi: B.R. Publishing.

Morris, C., & Fry, H. (2006). Enhancing educational research and development activity through small grant schemes: A case study. *International Journal of Academic Development, 11*(1), 43–56.

Mowles, G. (2011). *Rethinking management: Radical insights from the complexity sciences.* Abingdon: Routledge.

Nimmo, A., & Littlejohn, A. (2009). Encouraging learning innovation: Recognising and rewarding good practice. *Practice and Evidence of the Scholarship of Teaching and Learning in Higher Education, 4*(1), 41–55.

Roxå, T., & Mårtensson, K. (2013). *Significant networks for educational development.* Retrieved from http://www.konferenslund.se/pp/CEQ_Roxa_Martensson.pdf

Southwell, D., & Morgan, W. (2009). *Leadership and the impact of academic staff development and leadership development on student learning outcomes in higher education: A review of the literature.* Report for the Australian Learning and Teaching Council (ALTC), Queensland University of Technology, Strawberry Hills.

Sterman, J. D. (2006). Learning from evidence in a complex world. *American Journal of Public Health, 96*(3), 505–514. Retrieved from http://www.ncbi.nlm.nih.gov/pmc/articles/PMC1470513/

Wright, A., Hamilton, B., Mighty, J., Muirhead, B., & Scott, J. (2014a). *The Ontario universities' teaching evaluation toolkit: A feasibility study.* Report to the Ministry of Training, Colleges and Universities: Productivity and Innovation Fund Program, University of Windsor, Windsor.

Wright, A., Hamilton, B., Raffoul, J., & Marval, P. (2014b, July). *Embedded educational leadership initiatives at the university of Windsor: A ministry of training, colleges, and universities productivity and innovation fund initiative* (Contributors: T. Ackerson, D. Andrews, J. Bornais, J. Dixon, L. Gil, E. Kustra, S. McMurphy, M. Potter, & N. Timperio). Windsor: University of Windsor.

CHAPTER 10

Using Social Media to Learn from Conferences

Sue Beckingham

The value of attending conferences extends beyond the presentations, workshops and keynotes as they provide a wonderful space for networking and discussions about the topics shared. Taking this a step further, this networking also opens opportunities post event to continue the dialogues and potentially develop future collaborations.

However (speaking from personal experience) my best laid plans to reconnect with conference delegates have so often been thwarted when my memory has failed me and I cannot recall individual's names and I've lost the conference notepad I'd written valued names on, along with the delegate list. Over recent years I've overcome this by seizing the moment and connecting with individuals I meet at events right there and then through social media. My first quest is to see if the individual is on Twitter and connect with them there. I then follow this up (later that evening or as soon as I can) by finding them on LinkedIn and sending an invite to connect, with a brief message referring back to where we met and where appropriate what we had agreed to take forward. This helps the recipient recall who you are too, though your profile photo should help (a good reason why you should use a photo others will recognise on your social media profiles).

I've found these simple steps have provided a great way to extend my network and the means to keep in touch beyond the conference through direct messages via Twitter or LinkedIn messages.

© KONINKLIJKE BRILL NV, LEIDEN, 2018 | DOI 10.1163/9789004373013_010

1   Introduction

As an organiser of a conference it is hugely beneficial to capture the attention of your prospective audience months before the event itself. After all, you want to fill seats. During the conference, you want delegates to enjoy the event and encourage them to return the following year. Post conference, happy participants who go on to share the valuable knowledge they have gained through attending sessions and networking, can encourage others to attend the next event. For many years we have relied on word of mouth and email exchange; however, to some degree the impact has been limited. This chapter will explore how social media has augmented traditional approaches and provided spaces for interactive and engaging dialogues, creating a ripple effect that can share experiences far wider than ever before. Not only is this useful for the conference organiser, it provides new communication channels for prospective participants, the conference speakers, and also the wider public.

The chapter will consider:

– Preconference preparation
– During the conference
– Post conference
– Benefits for the participants
– Benefits for the speakers

Whilst the chapter won't provide a step by step guide on how to use specific tools, it does include a Social Media Toolkit which includes links to the tools mentioned in the chapter and for each one a link to the associated help pages.

2   Preconference Preparation

Using a blog as your conference website enables you to send out blog posts easily. You can use these to introduce topics that correspond with your conference timeline. Typically, this includes introducing the conference and its theme, the call for participation, how to register a place, information about the speakers, details of accommodation options, and maps and directions to the conference venue. This information can also be made available in static pages. An automated blog post can be used to send out a corresponding tweet as each post is published. This will take the title of the blogpost and add the URL link. Timesaving steps like these can be very useful for conference organisers.

2.1   *Conference Website*

At many institutions getting access to space on the university website can be problematic. It may be that you have to send Word documents to whoever is the gatekeeper of the site, and you are reliant on them adding to the web pages in a timely fashion. Updates can be delayed if they have other priorities. WordPress, which is a blogging tool, can be a quick and effective way of collating content about the conference. As with a website you can create multiple pages that are accessed by tabs. It is easy to add social media sharing buttons so that readers can share information quickly and easily with their own networks. You can embed the Twitter feed, which I will explain in more detail in the next section, but suffice to say this provides a live and visual presentation of what is being said about the conference. It is also easy to embed both video and audio using tools like YouTube, Vimeo, SoundCloud and AudioBoom (see Table 10.2). Audio tools are useful if you wish to record a series of podcasts.

2.2   *Twitter*

Twitter is a key tool in your social media toolbox and one you will use before, during, and after the conference. First of all, you need to set up a dedicated conference Twitter account. As the conference organising team is likely to be more than one person, it is also a good idea to set up a shared conference email address. That way you can share the username and password between the team (which may change in subsequent years) and means it is not down to one individual to use their personal email account. You will need an email address to create a new Twitter account (or any other social media channels you choose to use.)

When creating a new Twitter account, you will need to choose a username. Avoid using the year within this as this will become irrelevant quite quickly. An example might be @SocMedHE (the username for the Social Media for Learning Conference in Higher Education). You will also be asked to complete a short biography (referred to as a 'bio') for your account. This needs to be succinct as you are only allowed 160 characters plus the option to add a location and website. Ensure the bio includes the date of the event and a link to the conference website. This bio can then be updated each year. Your profile will also benefit from adding a logo in place of a photo that will be associated with the event. There is also an opportunity to add a banner image that will appear at the top of the Twitter profile page. Both the logo and banner need to align with your chosen branding and be similar if not the same as the image used as a header for the conference website. The reason for this is that viewers will find it easier to make visual connections when these are aligned. For example, the Social Media for Learning in Higher Education Conference uses the artwork from the conference website to create a matching Twitter avatar. Examples can be seen on the conference Twitter account at https://twitter.com/SocMedHE and the conference website at https://blogs.shu.ac.uk/socmedhe/

@SocMedHE

The 2nd Social Media for Learning in HE conference will be on 16th December 2016. #SocMedHE16

Sheffield, England
go.shu.ac.uk/socmedhe

FIGURE 10.1   *Social media for learning in higher education conference banner and logo*

Deciding upon the event hashtag is the next stage. This a short keyword preceded with #. For example, #SocMedHE16 was used for the 2016 conference mentioned above. When users search for this hashtag in Twitter (and other social media channels) it brings together a collection of tweets that contain the shared hashtag. The hashtag enables a form of 'searchable talk' (Zappavigna, 2013) that allows users to filter conversations related to the event.

When choosing a hashtag, be mindful that it needs to be succinct so that it doesn't use up too many characters (a tweet can be a maximum of 140 characters long). The hashtag needs to be memorable, so that users find it easy to type. It is also important to check that it is not already being used by others for other purposes. This can be done quickly and easily by entering it into the search box in Twitter. If it is being used, the search will bring up tweets containing the hashtag.

Once you have chosen your event hashtag, remember to make it prominent on your conference website and/or blog, along with the event Twitter account. The more people see links to the Twitter account and hashtag, the more likely they are to follow the Twitter account, save the hashtag and begin to interact with the conference conversations. You will then see the development of an active network that will go on to retweet the messages you are sharing. Not only will they interact with the event Twitter account but also those interested in attending. This can create quite a buzz before the event has even taken place.

One of the first key messages you will post via Twitter is a 'save this date' tweet, providing the title and date of the conference, a link to the conference site (blog or website) and the event hashtag. It is very important to remember to include the event hashtag in every tweet you send. Subsequent tweets might include the following:

— Call for participation
— Reminder of the closing date to submit papers
— Early bird booking
— Reminder when this early bird date is about to expire
— Links to the presenter abstracts, title of their session and their Twitter usernames (Note each session can be tweeted separately, perhaps spread out over a week or so depending on the size of the event and number of speakers)
— Information about how and where to book accommodation
— Further reminders about booking
— Images and information about the conference venue, along with directions by car, rail or air
— Things to do whilst in the conference venue location
— Closing date for bookings

In addition, you can tweet 'calls for action' – this is where you ask (potential) delegates questions to invite a response. Liking, retweeting and responding to answers, encourages further interactions with them and others who become interested in the event.

Where the conference includes invited keynote speakers, you may also want to consider including short videos (2–3 minutes) for the speakers to introduce themselves and the topic they will be discussing. These can be easily created by the speaker themselves using a webcam and YouTube; however, guidance should always be provided if required. What is considered easy for one could be quite stressful for another if the individual has never attempted this before. I would also add that it should be made clear with the speaker that this is an option they may choose to take up and that they would be supported in whatever way was required. For some this may be a set of instructions and how to register for a YouTube account. It is also important to send them a consent form to provide permission to use the media created on your conference site and via social media.

At the very least it is valuable to share photos of the keynote speakers when posting information about them. Rogers (2014), who is the Data Editor for Twitter, analysed the content of over 2 million tweets and found that the number of retweets was increased by 35% when it contained a photo, 28% when it contained a video, and 19% when it contained a quote. You can see multimedia can add impact and result in wider publicity for your event.

2.3   Eventbrite

This is a useful website that can help you promote your conference and also capture registrations. This is particularly useful if you do not have a central events team. For free events there is no cost, however for paying events, there is a commission to pay. Details can be found on the Eventbrite website (see Table 10.2). One of the advantages of using this site is that it prompts users to share the event through their social media networks.

Eventbrite includes a feature that enables delegates to sign up for individual sessions within the conference. Each session page can be set to accept a maximum number of people and will provide an alert when the session is full. As the organiser you will receive a list of the people who have signed up for the event along with their email addresses. There is also the facility for individuals to submit questions about the event.

2.4   Registration

Along with the usual key information you need to gather (for example: delegate name, role, institution, email, dietary requirements) it is very useful to add an additional field to capture the delegate's Twitter username. This can then be included in the participant list and will help people to make connections and extend their network prior to the event. It is also helpful to include the username below the delegate's name on name badges. Quite often it seems, individuals use 'alternative' names instead of their own. For example, Prof Steve Wheeler, a prominent tweeter goes by the name of @timbuckteeth. Delegates can capture the Twitter names as they are networking and for some their names can be a conversation starter!

2.5   Building Relationships with the Speakers and Delegates

It is useful to collate the Twitter usernames of your speakers. These can be provided as a list within Twitter to group the tweets from your list of Twitter accounts. A link can then be shared to this list within a tweet and on the conference site. This will help everyone make connections more easily and contribute to the development of their personal networks. See https://twitter.com/SocMedHE/lists for examples.

Keeping an eye on the event hashtag is an important task so that you can react to the tweets people make. Where possible it is helpful to have more than one person from the conference team to do this. The designated 'Tweeters' can reply to questions raised, retweet and like tweets, and generate discussion by posting questions or creating a Twitter poll. Closer to the event people can be asked to tweet where they are coming from, how they are travelling, what they are bringing with them etc. The conference ALTC led by the Association of Learning Technology introduced a 'green theme' in 2016 and encouraged participants to tweet photos of green objects they encountered on the journey. Whilst just light- hearted fun, this was very popular and provided opportunities for people to interact with each other as they travelled. Some discovered they were on the same train!

Where speakers do not have a Twitter account it can be helpful to explain to them the advantages of using Twitter (see further into this chapter, in the section on 'Benefits for Speakers'). Whilst it is always an individual choice whether to join any social network site, gentle encouragement can often be welcomed as can support in getting started. From experience as a conference organiser I have since been thanked for introducing colleagues to Twitter.

With these suggestions in place you will soon be sharing a variety of content via Twitter using text, images and potentially video and audio too. Asking people to retweet your tweets (often abbreviated as 'please RT!') does exactly that, as it does encourage retweeting.

3   During the Conference

3.1   *Event Hashtag*
Make sure this is promoted well. It should appear in the conference pack and ideally be printed on posters displayed in all rooms used during the conference. Introduce the hashtag and the conference Twitter account in the opening talk in a slide of its own and add the hashtag to each subsequent slide. Encourage delegates to tweet and tell them the aim is to get the hashtag trending – the more people that tweet the further the messages will reach! For those new to Twitter is can be very motivating to be told to tweet and not put away your mobile phones (Semple & McAfee, 2012).

3.2   *Tweeting Key Information*
Use the conference Twitter account to post useful housekeeping information. Delegates will soon realise this is where to go to check up on things and can use Twitter to ask questions. Answering questions publicly often helps others too with the same questions. Where needed, individual specific Q&As can be continued as direct messages or email.

Promote each of the sessions along with the name of the presenter(s), their Twitter user name(s) and a link to their abstract on the conference website or blog. These tweets can be pre-scheduled prior to the event using a dashboard like Tweetdeck or Hootsuite. Using this tool allows you to set aside some time to compose the tweets you want to send and to select a time for them to then be automatically posted (see Table 10.2 for more information about these tools).

3.3 *Video*

There are a number of options available to capture a video version of an event. For some conferences only the keynote speakers are recorded and this may be done by the conference organiser's technical team. There are now a variety of app based tools that can be used directly from a mobile phone and increasingly these are used by participants during events. As with photographs there is an etiquette to follow. Where the organisers are filming the speakers, they should seek prior permission to do so. In the event a speaker specifically asks not to be filmed and/or photographed, then it is very important these wishes are conveyed to everyone present at the conference prior to their talk. It is always good practice to warn delegates that filming is going to take place and that a photographer may be taking photos, so that they have the option of not being part of this. Equally it is helpful to remind delegates to seek permission to film any sessions they attend.

A video can be captured and easily shared on YouTube or Vimeo after the event. An increasingly popular approach is livestreaming so that external or virtual participants can watch the speakers live. This can be done by using Google Hangouts on Air or Periscope via mobile technology. It is worth investing in a tripod or portable stand as it can become quite tiring on the arms holding your device up for prolonged periods.

4 Post Conference

4.1 *Curation*

Storify is a useful online tool that allows curated content to be shared via a variety of social media as a 'story'. A popular method is to curate all the tweets within a short period that contain a specific hashtag. The tool enables these tweets to be gathered and transferred to a storyboard. There is an option to display the tweets in newest or oldest order. Save and publish the long list of tweets as a post. The link to the Storify post can then be shared via Twitter or any other communication channel. With a little more time you can add context to the storyboard by adding text boxes between the saved tweets. The resulting 'story' can be displayed as a list or as a slideshow. Once published, the URL link can be shared on the website and through social media posts. An example can be found here https://storify.com/suebecks/19th-annual-seda-conference-sedaconf-seda.

4.2 *Vox Pops*

Short videos can be captured to garner feedback about sessions during or just after the conference, and then shared post event. When uploaded to YouTube or Vimeo the short videos can be shared via social media and embedded on the conference website.

4.3   *Speaker Presentations*

These can be gathered from the speakers and added to the conference site as PowerPoint presentations which can then be downloaded to view. Alternatively, the presentation can be uploaded to SlideShare. It is then possible to embed slideshows which add a visual dimension to the website or blog. There are two options here:

1   Encourage speakers to upload their presentation to their own SlideShare account and share the link.
2   Create a conference SlideShare account and ask speakers to send the presentation file so that you can add to this account.

Once this has been done, Twitter and other social networks can be used to share a link to this information. Be sure to include the conference hashtag as this will help people find these new resources.

5   Benefits for the Participants

I've talked quite a bit about the value of Twitter and hashtags. From my own perspective, the first thing I do when a conference catches my eye is to check to see if there is a conference hashtag. This gives me an indication of who is talking about the event. I then look to see what social spaces the conference is using – usually Twitter but sometimes a Facebook group is included – and I will then follow the conversations in these social spaces. This then provides me with updates as and when the conference organisers tweet out information. I will also save the hashtag as a search and keep a watch on this.

5.1   *Making Connections*

Once you have Twitter in place you can start to engage in dialogues by tweeting that you have submitted a paper or booked on the event, which often results in a reply from someone who has just done the same. Doing this allows delegates to not only see who else will be attending the event but also provides the opportunity to prearrange shared travel arrangements, get advice on local accommodation, and to arrange meetups on arrival. As the event gets closer, conversations develop. Of course, to be part of these shared conversations, you need to follow the conference hashtag and add this to your own tweets so that they can be found by others (who may not yet follow you). Those following the tweets containing the hashtag can then choose to make new connections with those tweeting.

5.2   *Tweeting at the Conference*

At most conferences it is now accepted practice for participants to tweet about the event. These tweets tend to mainly focus on the presentations and workshops people attend. Tweets might include:

– quotes from the speakers
– photos of visual slides or where the font is large enough to be snapped clearly
– links to papers, books, websites or other resources shared by the speakers and delegates
– discussion about the presentations/workshops attended
– asking a question about a topic
– giving feedback about a presentation

Twitter names are not always easy to find. It is very helpful to provide conference attendees with a delegate list that includes this information. However quite often now such lists are only made available online and not as a printed list, so even if the Twitter names have been captured, delegates have to go looking online for this information. Presenters can help the audience by adding their Twitter handle to each of their slides. This can be placed in one of the corners and pointed out by the presenter at the start of the presentation.

For some participants, tweeting is used as a form of notetaking. As tweets are public this can also be useful for others. Individuals reading the tweets can 'like' the tweets as a way to save them to read later. Tweets need to be succinct so taking photos of slides as they are presented can be a useful form of recall, when reviewing these tweets after the event.

Whilst at many events Twitter is now an accepted form of communication, consideration should be given to good Twitter (and other social media) etiquette. There are a few things to consider:

– When taking photos of people speaking, do seek their permission. The conference organisers may have already sought permission from speakers, but it is courteous to check.
– When tweeting quotes, ensure that these are always attributed to the speaker. Ideally use the person's Twitter user name or if this is not known search for it (using the search box in Twitter or check the tweets of others who may know it and already have tweeted using this. Failing that, use the person's full name. Place quotes in speech marks.
– Differentiate your own opinions from the speakers.
– When discussing the event through tweeting, always be polite and respectful.

– If someone asks for their work not to be shared, then respect that request.
– Be professional and remember anyone can view the tweets.
– Do remember to PUT YOUR PHONE ON SILENT! No-one wants to hear the pings you may receive every 30 seconds,

5.3   *Following Tweets*

You can keep track of the tweets participants make by searching for the conference hashtag and saving this. This will curate all the tweets that include the hashtag. To save a Twitter search enter the hashtag into the search box. At the top of the results page, click on 'more options' and then 'save this search'. The next time you click the search box you will see a pop-up menu which will display this and any other saved searches you may have.

For anyone new to Twitter, Table 10.1 provides an explanation of some of the terms that are frequently used.

TABLE 10.1   *Twitter terms*

mention	where the username is included in a tweet e.g. @suebecks
RT	retweet, sharing something someone has already tweeted
H/T	hat tip (acknowledge someone else)
M/T	(slightly) modified retweet
tweetup	a physical meetup of Tweeters
hashtag	#keyword preceded by # that is searchable

5.4   *Preparation*

If you are going to tweet at an event then you will find it useful if you have done a little preparation. My suggestions would be:

– Check your own Twitter account – have you got a clear bio on your profile and a photo? You are more likely to be followed or retweeted if others can identify who you are.
– Find out what the event hashtag is and make a note of this. There is nothing more frustrating than to be merrily tweeting away and finding you have either not included the hashtag or you've been using the wrong one.
– Consider the sessions you are likely to go to and identify what the speakers' Twitter names are in advance. (There are now often included in the programme)

– If you want to be super organised you may choose to follow the speakers and
  add them to a named list.

5.5   *Virtual Participation*

In some cases it may be that you cannot actually attend an event due to work
commitments or lack of funding. It is possible, however, to engage with the
conference as a virtual participant using social media. It may be that you
tried this some time ago and did not have a very active experience. Research
undertaken by Ross et al. (2011) that involved the analysis of tweets during
three international conferences in 2009 found that the Twitter activity
represented multiple monologues and just a few 'intermittent discontinuous,
loosely joined dialogues' between users. This aligns with my early experience
in 2011. I was unable to attend the SEDA Conference taking place in Edinburgh
but was thrilled to find that a hashtag had been shared by someone I knew who
was attending. From memory, I think there were only half a dozen tweeting
so I confess I was not anticipating an immersive experience, but I was keen
to pursue this mode of communication and encouraged those active to keep
me informed about the event. Their tweets gave me a flavour of the key points
emerging from the presentations that they were attending. As a result of this I
shared a number of interactions with Dr David Walker. I was able to respond to
his tweets and this developed into a dialogue. I had the opportunity to question
or add my own views.

An unexpected outcome from this conference was that our Twitter
discussions led to us discussing a conference proposal for the next SEDA
conference. We went on to plan this, using Twitter direct messages, some
email exchanges, and one telephone conversation. Our proposal was accepted
and David and I met for the first time at the next conference at which we
presented. Our presentation 'Using social media to develop your own personal
learning network' was shared via SlideShare, LinkedIn and Twitter and to date
has received over 17,000 views (Beckingham & Walker, 2011). Subsequent SEDA
conferences have seen a steady growth in participants tweeting both at the
event and those virtually contributing (Beckingham, 2011). These conversations
are often referred to as the conference backchannel.

Another example of virtual participation I've experienced was when a tweet
chat was planned into a conference workshop. Andrew Middleton and Sue
Moron-Garcia encouraged participants physically at the workshop to tweet
their answers and also invited those following the conference hashtag to join
in the synchronous tweet chat. An additional bespoke hashtag was used to
filter these tweets. In the physical chat participants made use of post-its to
answer the questions. Those also engaging in the open tweet chat took photos
of these and added them to the tweets. Five questions had been planned and

pre-scheduled using Tweetdeck to tweet at timed intervals during the session. This allowed the facilitators to focus on the participants in the room, but still allowed the opportunity to tweet a few photos of the physical space they were in. An unexpected outcome of this workshop was the blog posts written by the virtual participants who had welcomed the opportunity to be involved in the workshop.

A third example of virtual participation is the brilliant initiative called 'Virtually Connecting' created by Dr Maha Bali and Rebecca Hogue (2015a). Like many they had realised through their networks that there were valuable conversations to be had using Twitter, including virtual participation at conferences. They decided to take this a step further by using emerging technologies to bring a visual element to these interactions. Their innovative approach actually started as a pilot. Maha who had initially planned to attend and present at the 'Emerging Technologies for Online Learning' in the US, was unable to make the event. As Rebecca was going to be onsite, they came up with a plan to enable Maha to attend virtually. Rebecca not only organised the conversations that had been pre-scheduled with speakers, she also found opportunities to create informal gatherings to 'hang out' with participants at the event. Using their own mobile technology and Google Hangouts on Air, the pair engaged in conversations, bringing in some of the presenters to talk about their conference experience and their own presentations (Hogue & Bali, 2015b). What made this approach extra special was that they had also invited some other virtual participants to join these conversations. Google Hangouts on Air is a video conferencing tool that is similar to Skype and Facetime enabling small groups of people to see and talk to each other. The conversation is automatically saved and posted to YouTube. This means it can be watched post event as well as live during the event.

Bali et al. (2016) refer to Virtually Connecting as "a connected learning volunteer movement that enlivens virtual conference experiences by partnering those that are at the conference with virtual participants that cannot attend". Maha and Rebecca have reached out to an interconnected community and developed a team of volunteers across the globe, who now contributes to the organisation of 'Virtually Connecting' (VC) conversations as onsite or virtual buddies.

As Twitter is used as a conduit to share forthcoming VC supported events, I quickly picked up opportunities to listen in to the live streamed VC events. One of my first experiences of being involved onsite was at ALTC in 2015 (see the Playlist for #altc here: http://www.tiny.cc/altcvc). I've since volunteered to be an onsite buddy at #SocMedHE15 with keynote Eric Stoller and ALTC in 2016 with keynotes Josie Fraser and Jane Secker. What is so fascinating, are the choices this model offers. Participants can be active (onsite or virtually), or simply listen in (real time or through the recording). This makes it very inclusive and allows those new to this concept to find their feet and preferred mode of engagement.

You can find out more about this community via the website at http://virtuallyconnecting.org/ and https://twitter.com/VConnecting.

6   Benefits for the Speakers

6.1   *Building Your Network*
Having a Twitter account means that when the organiser tweets out links to the presenters' abstracts they can include their username. This provides the presenter with a notification alert and they can then retweet the tweet and share this with their network. By including the conference hashtag anyone following this can also read the tweets. People interested in the abstract are then likely to check out the presenter's Twitter account and may decide to follow them. The presenter then has the option to follow them back. Key to this is the content of the presenter's and the tweeter's respective bios.

– What does the Twitter bio tell others?
– Do they have mutual interests?

Twitter accounts where the user has not completed their bio and/or not bothered to upload a photo are less likely to be followed than those that have. So it makes sense to provide a clear bio and where applicable include a link to a blog, website and perhaps a LinkedIn profile.

6.2   *Interacting with Your Audience*
Twitter can provide opportunities to add additional dimensions to an event. For example: presenter and audience interactions. With some preparation tweets can be pre-scheduled to integrate questions, polls or feedback. In addition, those following the conference hashtag can engage in interconnected audience interactions; in person and virtual interactions; and a multiplicity of pre and post event interactions (Lancaster & Beckingham, 2016).

6.3   *Disseminating Your Work*
During the event presenters can tweet details of their session and alert people to the location. There is nothing wrong with promoting your own presentation. Indeed, people will be grateful to have this information signposted as it can help them plan their conference schedule.

It is useful to participants if presenters make known their Twitter name during the talk: this can be included both on the cover slide and subsequent slides. That way participants can include this in their tweets and the presenter will receive notifications of any mentions. This in turn allows others to catch on to the presenter's Twitter name and follow them. After a presentation the presenter can check any notifications they may have and respond to these. In some cases this can lead to interesting discussions about the topic they have shared and potentially lead to future collaborations between colleagues with shared mutual interests.

Another useful social media tool is SlideShare. This is a space where users can upload PowerPoint presentations, infographics and PDF documents. Uploading presentations in this space provides an easy way to share work. There is the option of retaining full copyright or giving the work a Creative Commons Licence. There's a variety to choose from and it is recommended to visit the Creative Commons website to get further information (Creative Commons, n.d.). As an open educator, I have always gone for the option that explicitly indicates that others can reuse my work with attribution for non-commercial use. It is possible to tweet a link or share the SlideShare presentation via other social networks. It is also possible to easily embed the SlideShare presentation into a LinkedIn profile or within a blog post. This way a wider online network can see the presentation when visiting these social spaces.

7   A Social Media Toolkit

It can be dangerous to refer to specific digital and social media since as new apps and software are continuously emerging and others may fall by the wayside, however, it is hoped this will give a flavour of what has been used to good effect. Table 10.2 includes the social media tools referred to in this chapter, along with links to the associated online guidance to use them.

When looking to use social media tools that are new to you, it can be helpful to visit the support pages of the tool you are planning to use. They have detailed 'how to' guides including screenshots and step by step instructions, which explain how to create an account. You can then dip in and out, as and when questions arise.

It would be an omission if it was not mentioned that social media and any digital technology has its glitches from time to time. An organiser would be well advised to include colleagues with technical experience within the organising team. Having this support can relieve unwanted anxiety while providing opportunities to develop new skills. Drawing upon student volunteers is

TABLE 10.2   *A social media toolkit*

Tool name	Website	Help
AudioBoom	https://audioboom.com/	https://audioboom.zendesk.com/hc/en-us
EventBrite	https://www.eventbrite.com/	https://www.eventbrite.co.uk/support
Facebook	https://www.facebook.com/	https://en-gb.facebook.com/help/
Google Hangouts	https://hangouts.google.com/	https://support.google.com/hangouts/
Hootsuite	https://hootsuite.com	https://hootsuite.com/en-gb/help
LinkedIn	https://www.linkedin.com/	https://www.linkedin.com/help/linkedin
Periscope	https://www.periscope.tv/	https://help.periscope.tv/
SoundCloud	https://soundcloud.com/	http://help.soundcloud.com/
Storify	https://storify.com/	https://storify.uservoice.com/
Tweetdeck	https://tweetdeck.twitter.com/	https://support.twitter.com/articles/20169620#
Twitter	https://twitter.com/	https://support.twitter.com/
Vimeo	https://vimeo.com	https://help.vimeo.com/hc/en-us
WordPress	https://wordpress.com/	https://en.support.wordpress.com/
YouTube	https://www.youtube.com	https://support.google.com/youtube/

another consideration. Do not make the mistake of completely handing over the reigns as it is important that a communication strategy is considered. A team approach is best to share the responsibility.

Finally, please do not jump in with both feet and assume you need to take on all of the suggestions in this chapter in one go! Try one approach at a time. My recommendation would be to start with Twitter. It's an ideal way to share short messages and can be deployed using your desktop, laptop, tablet or smartphone.

In summary, social media provides an extension to your conference website and can help to promote your event. It allows you to communicate with delegates ahead of the conference, during, and afterwards. As an organiser you can collect ongoing feedback and respond to questions.

Delegates and speakers can start to make connections and engage in dialogue in advance of the event. This in itself can help to build the conference community. Conversations that begin before the conference, have the potential to continue when delegates meet face to face. Social media provides spaces to continue discussions way beyond the event. The networks that develop as a result can become advocates of future conferences. The benefits are of course mutual. As the call for speakers goes out, this network is able to receive advance notifications, and also share this with others. Successful submissions will be celebrated.

Social media has the potential to keep the conference conversation going long after the event. As more embrace its use, the rewards will follow. Delegates and speakers can go on to reflect on their conference experience, enabling more people to learn from the rich array of presentations, research papers and workshops. This has to be a valuable addition to our continued professional development.

References

Bali, M., Caines, A., DeWaard, H., & Hogue, R. J. (2016). Ethos and practice of a connected learning movement: Interpreting virtually connecting through alignment with theory and survey results. *Online Learning, 20*(4). Retrieved from https://olj.onlinelearningconsortium.org/index.php/olj/article/view/965

Beckingham, S. (2011). The impact of Twitter and its new relationship with the SEDA community. *SEDA Educational Developments, 12*(4). Retrieved from http://www.seda.ac.uk/resources/files/publications_127_Ed%20Devs%2012.4%20 FINAL.pdf

Beckingham, S., & Walker, D. (2011). *Using social media to develop your own personal learning network*. Retrieved from http://www.slideshare.net/suebeckingham/using-social-media-to-develop-your-own-personal-learning-network

Creative Commons. (n.d.). *About the licenses: What our licenses do*. Retrieved from https://creativecommons.org/licenses/

Hogue, R., & Bali, M. (2015a). Beyond Twitter: Virtually connecting at conferences. *The Chronicle of Higher Education* [blog post]. Retrieved from http://www.chronicle.com/ blogs/profhacker/beyond-twitter-virtually-connecting-at-conferences/60339

Hogue, R., & Bali, M. (2015b). Expanding and extending conversations at #altc via @vconnecting. *#ALTC Blog*. Retrieved from https://altc.alt.ac.uk/blog/2015/09/ expanding-and-extending-conversations-at-altc-via-vconnecting/

Lancaster, S., & Beckingham, S. (2016). *The four dimensional conference: Using social media at conferences*. Retrieved from https://www.heacademy.ac.uk/blog/four-dimensional-conference-using-social-media-conferences

Rogers, S. (2014). *What fuels a Tweet's engagement?* Retrieved from
   https://blog.twitter.com/2014/what-fuels-a-tweets-engagement

Ross, C., Terras, M., Warwick, C., & Welsh, A. (2011). Enabled backchannel: Conference
   Twitter use by digital humanists. *Journal of Documentation, 67*(2), 214–237.

Semple, E., & McAfee, A, (2012). *Organizations don't Tweet, people do: A manager's
   guide to the social web.* Chichester: John Wiley & Sons Ltd.

Zappavigna, M. (2012). *Discourse of Twitter and social media: How we use language to
   create affiliation on the web.* London: Continuum International Publishing Group.

CHAPTER 11

Building on Your Learning as a Conference Designer and Provider through Evaluation, Feedback and Review

Alice L. E. V. Cassidy and Celia Popovic

On the flight home from a teaching and learning conference held at a mid-sized Canadian university, I passed the time by doing an analysis of the conference participant list (back in the days when such lists were provided). It turned out that 60 people from the host institution attended the conference. There were 11 from our university in attendance. In fact, there were more people from that university's biology department at the conference than there were from my rather large university. It became clear from this simple head count that one objective in hosting a conference is to get your own people to attend. The numbers are rather astounding when you get it right.

When we hosted, we used some of our own funds to allow for a reduced registration fee for our own folks. That year, over 100 people from our institution attended.

To maximize the value of this significant jump in attendance, we held post-conference sessions at which people discussed their impressions of the conference. Also, some people gave reprised versions of the sessions they had led. This particular teaching and learning organization was extremely supportive of the advancement of educational development across the country, so the fact that significantly more of our people knew of it was a real

shot in the arm for us. In subsequent years, our people continued to attend
the conference, though never in the numbers that we saw when we hosted.
GARY POOLE

1   Introduction

In earlier chapters, we focused on aspects of conference focus, format, and
contexts. The key goal of this chapter is to address the multi-faceted ways of
collecting information, reflecting and acting upon these data for a conference
you have just been involved in organizing, and identifying ways to improve
in the future. We will consider ways to maximize learning from conferences
including the use of evaluation, feedback and review of this information.

We will describe suggested steps that take place before, during, and/or after
the conference. You and your team may be organizing an annual conference
at your institution or you might be hosting a conference that then takes
place elsewhere in another year. In either scenario, the learning, perhaps
documented in some kind of summary, or report from organizing one event
can be applied to work on other small- or large-scale events in which you
and colleagues find yourselves involved. A key question is: How best can you
make use of evaluation, feedback, and your review of these to make each new
iteration the best it can be?

Often, conferences that are associated with a society are designed by a new
team or committee each time, as these events, be they annual or less frequent,
are hosted by different post-secondary institutions each time. Ideally, each
new organizing committee builds on the work of previous committees so as
to avoid making any mistakes that could have been predicted, moves forward
to make the event the best it can be, and shows participants of previous years
that their input has been heard, and where appropriate, incorporated. As a
member or leader of such a new team or committee, you might be working in
liaison with a representative of a national or international board or executive
for guidelines and assistance.

Many institutions offer their own conference annually. The team responsible
for making it a success each time needs to consider various aspects, including
keeping it fresh. For either kind of conference, a report on the experience is a
great way to keep everything in one place for future reference.

Imagine that a conference that you organized has just ended. Your first
response might well be, "Phew, we did it!" And it is time for a well-earned break.
Your second response may be, "How did it go?" followed by "How can we find
out?" This may include the impressions of you and your team as well as those
of the participants and others involved. You will want evidence of course, and

this is where various kinds of information are important, to enable you to put it all together and review the conference.

Let's go back to the beginning. As you embark on conference planning, what are your criteria for success? How will you know if you have met some or all of them? Be clear about the intention of the conference. There may be multiple aims, some of which may be implied. As a conference organizer spend some time identifying what success will look like for you and your team. In some cases, this may be attracting a certain number of participants, or creating a climate for some form of change. Whatever your goal, it is important to know how you will recognize when you have met it. Below we provide some guidance.

2   Evaluation

2.1   *Evaluation by Participants*

Most conferences ask participants to say how it went from their perspective.

Before the conference: Decide what questions to ask. Do the responses to your questions serve a purpose? Consider how you will summarize the data; this may help determine the format or content of questions. A mix of Likert and open-ended style is usually best. Is there a 'stock' evaluation form that is kept the same each year? Or are you starting from 'scratch'? Review any previous evaluation forms to determine their applicability and make amendments as necessary. Aim for a balance between obtaining the information you need to measure success, and asking as few questions as possible. The shorter the evaluation form the more likely it is that people will complete it. See http://tinyurl.com/ycbea7y8 for a template form you may wish to adapt for your own use.

Ivie and Czujka (2007) provide tips on writing questions and responses to ensure the respondent answers the question you meant to ask. They also discuss the length of surveys and other tips to increase response rate. A detailed overview of question design, including a review of literature is presented by Krosnick and Presser (2010).

If your survey will be completed electronically, there are several considerations. Is there an upper limit to the number of words on open-ended responses? If so, is this appropriate? Does the response to one question lead to related ones? Do you have access to an online survey software provided by your institution? If so, this may impact the possible design. Once completed, responses and other data from surveys done in this way can often be summarized at the click of a button. It is crucial to test your survey, by yourself and others who were not involved in the design, to ensure it works correctly. Leave time for this as well as the possible ensuing fine-tuning.

During the conference: Prepare participants. Tell them that evaluation will take place, noting when and how. Make a note of it on the conference website right from the start. Be very clear about when the evaluation, if electronic, will be emailed out, and the deadline for completion. We have seen success with offering one or more prizes, drawn at random, from those who complete the evaluation. If the survey is done in hard copy at the event, the prize can be something physical; if it is done electronically, consider a gift card or another electronic prize.

Mention the participant evaluation in the opening comments and frequently during the conference. If there is an electronic or hard copy conference programme, note it there. Make it clear that evaluation is important and it will be used to inform conference design in the future.

If you are using a hard copy, include it in the conference package. Consider providing time during the closing plenary for people to complete the form. Though an online form allows easier and quicker collection and summary of response data, it may not yield the same quantity of responses as when using an electronic form, unless you take active measures to maximize completion. Some tactics that encourage engagement were mentioned earlier such as competitions or prizes. You may also want to consider response vs completion rate. Some online survey tools provide a guide to required numbers. See one example at: http://fluidsurveys.com/university/response-rate-statistics-online-surveys-aiming/.

After the conference: Whether your survey was provided as hard copy or online, remind participants about it, to give yourself a chance to collect any remaining responses. For electronic surveys, email participants a few days after the conference and again a week later. Use this as an opportunity to thank participants and presenters for attending. Late completion of surveys may have an advantage in that responses may be more thoughtful than those given at the immediate close of the conference. Make plans to summarize your data promptly after the deadline. Consider whether it would be appropriate to share the results or excerpts of them with those who contributed to the survey. If so, this is a good way to 'walk the talk', showing that you care about participants' time and voice. It may be appropriate to include a summary of the evaluation findings in a conference report.

2.2 *Evaluation by Organizers and Others*

Involve organizers and volunteers in evaluating the process; although this may not be commonly done, it is recommended. Provide an opportunity for members of the organizing team, and perhaps others involved, to comment on how the conference went from their perspective, and in a safe, anonymous manner, as this can be highly informative. Other commentators may include sponsors (if applicable), administrators, the keynote speaker, and volunteers among others.

3   Feedback

Feedback is usually less formal than evaluation and can take a variety of forms, including written and oral comments that may be anecdotal and/or solicited.

Different kinds of feedback can be collected before, during or after the event.

Before the conference: As conference organizers, we have been asked questions by potential presenters and participants as early as the first conference announcement. These early questions can be very revealing, perhaps indicating something on the website that is in need of clarification for example. There could be small or large errors that you and your team overlooked, but now prospective registrants notice. It is important to post a contact email on the conference website; be sure to monitor it right from the start.

During the conference: Organizers should take the opportunity to chat with participants at breaks, receptions and when walking from one venue to another. Keep it light, but be clear who you are. Ask questions such as "How's it going?" "Is this your first time at this conference?" It can be easier to do this if the organizers wear a badge or some form of indication that they are one of the organizers. One of us, while at a prominent conference's opening reception, was asked a question such as this by the organizer. After expressing frustration at our fellow delegates' lack of response to our efforts in trying to strike up conversations, the organizer was genuinely concerned and planned to consider ways to encourage conversation in the future.

Some comments may be overly negative, so try not to be too sensitive. Alice had an interesting experience at a conference she had previously organized. Alice says: I found myself at a table with one of the organizers and one of the most vocal, negative participants I have ever met. The latter was talking at length about all the things they thought were wrong with the conference. I knew from experience that this person complained about most things. The organizer likely did not know this detail. Eventually, the organizer got up and left. I chatted to them later to give context about this unfortunate individual. I hope it made the organizer feel better and not to take it personally.

After the conference: You may receive informal emails, both negative and positive from participants. These are in addition to the formal post conference evaluation. Be sure to keep and summarize the information for future use, including it in your event summary. If any of it seems irrelevant to future events, make note, but we still suggest including all of it.

3.1   Solicited Feedback from Key Players

Before the conference: Consider ahead of time who you hope to collect impressions from, when and how. Decide if this needs to be kept anonymous or if this is not necessary.

3.2   During or after the Conference

Ask presenters over coffee or lunch how their sessions went, and which sessions they have most enjoyed. Speak with the keynote speaker(s), ask them about their impression of the conference. Most conferences are so fast-paced that it may not be feasible to meet while it is all happening so consider meeting up shortly afterwards. For example, you could engage them in an informal conversation through email, or arrange a Skype or phone meeting after the event, or you could ask them to complete a brief written form.

After the conference: consider emailing all the presenters after the conference, thanking them for their participation and asking them for their feedback. This may be in the form of two questions – tell us one thing we did exceptionally well and one thing we could do better next time.

Decide whether to solicit feedback on individual sessions. Presenters can be asked to gather the feedback themselves if you are not interested in seeing the individual results. This saves on administration and is particularly appropriate when presenters come from a range of institutions. With in-house conferences it may be relevant for the organizers to see the feedback. In this case decide if you wish to ask participants to complete a form after every session or include questions in the general evaluation. Chapter 5 provides examples of feedback forms that organizers or session leaders can adapt for use.

3.3   Other Kinds of Data

Look at participant numbers. This is likely to include not only the total number of individuals, but also their affiliations, job roles, or other information. With an internal conference, for instance, you may have been aiming for a balanced representation from across the institution. With a national or international conference, you may have been hoping to attract more participants and/or presenters from your home institution, as suggested by the anecdote at the start of this chapter.

Perhaps you had the specific aim of attracting a particular group of colleagues who previously had not engaged. Whatever your aim, did you achieve it? If the answer is yes: congratulations. Whether you succeeded or not, consider how it came to be. If this did not happen, what might you change next time? Some conferences rely on presenters from a variety of geographical locations or institutions, especially if they have advertised the event as being 'international', for instance. The anecdote describes how, returning from the same conference that the writer will now host at their institution, they chose to attract folks from their own institution by being able to offer a discount on the registration fees, thanks to sponsorship from upper administration. This story also underscores the advantage of attending the very conference you know you will organize the following year.

4   Review

Take all available information from the conference, reflect on what worked well and what might have been changed for better effect. Wait for a couple of days after the end of the conference, then ask your team for their reflections. If feasible, hold a meeting to reflect on the various forms of data collection discussed above.

Use all of the findings for two inter-related actions: write a report about the conference for use by others who will coordinate it in the future, and keep notes for yourself for other large-scale learning events you might organize in the future.

Negative or positive, all the information you collected is invaluable in improving and enhancing for next time. What about comments you do not like? Not all input is welcome, such as with the experiences described above. However, even the most seemingly unfair comments may contain a grain of truth. You may not be able to address every issue, but can you identify a theme that runs through the negative comments? Was the venue inappropriate, was this due to a structural unchangeable issue such as the room design, or was it due to a temporary unavoidable issue such as an isolated maintenance issue? Try to tease out aspects that can be changed and those that cannot. If you are organizing a similar event in the future, change the issues that are within your control and either ignore or apologise for those you cannot. If the conference now changes hands and institutions, pass along the information to future organizers.

Are there common themes? Are you hearing similar criticisms and or praise from a range of people? As with any research, the larger the number of data points the more robust the findings. If the conference organizers and presenters both say there was a problem with the projection facilities, this is likely to be an issue. If only one person comments, then it may not be significant. You will have outliers, just as with many forms of data collection.

4.1   *Topics to Consider*
4.1.1   Venue
Reflect on the space used for the conference. Whether you held the conference in a hotel or at your institution, would you use the same venue again? If so, what were the positive aspects that made it a success? Knowing why something was good can be as useful as knowing the reverse. If you know that the reason the

space worked was due to a particular aspect of architecture or location may help you to determine a suitable alternative if this is not available next time.

Was the venue easy to reach? Did people have difficulty in finding it? Was it accessible by all? What were the parking or transport arrangements and were they suitable?

Consider the plenary and break out rooms. Again, were they appropriate and if so why? If the conference grows in future will the same rooms be appropriate? Were there any problems reported by participants or others that could be addressed in the future? If they were not suitable what was the problem?

4.1.2   Catering

Consider value for money, ease of organization, service, and how much of what you paid for was used/consumed. Including details in a report can be useful for the next group to organize the same conference, even if the conference is held in a different part of the world. One example is to look at the number of meals ordered in relation to the number of registrants. If there was a lot of uneaten food, the next group might order less. Another option for the next group is to include a few questions in the registration about which events (that involve food) participants plan to attend. This information can be very valuable for food orders. At a conference in British Columbia, many fewer people attended the opening reception than the number who registered for the conference. Large quantities of smoked salmon, sushi, and other west coast specialties went uneaten. Asking registrants if they planned to come to the event might have prevented this extra cost (and potential waste of good food.) This is really tricky – we regularly have far fewer people attend than say they will – even with a reminder, but on the other hand no one wants to run out of food. For something that is more a courtesy than dinner, we often order food for about 2/3 the number who say they will attend. Even if they all turn up not everyone will eat and some may eat very little.

If you will not organize the same conference again, you may well be able to use your experience for a future event in which you are involved. Over time you may build up a relationship with caterers, printers and others, which helps when organizing another event, knowing what to expect from previous work and being able to fine-tune each time. Building rapport with a caterer can also help ease your mind amid a great many planning details needed for a conference or other large- scale event.

4.1.3   Presentations

As discussed above, some organizers solicit feedback from participants for each session. If this is relevant, review the feedback to determine what, if anything needs to be changed next time. Perhaps you tried some alternative session formats. Did they work? Did presenters stick to time and do what they said they would do? Do the presenters need more guidance next time to make the sessions work? Seek feedback from the presenters as well. Did they find the format and timing appropriate? Do you need to make sessions longer or shorter next time? Finally, if you collected feedback on presentations, it is fair to send them along to the presenter, in hard copy or electronically, depending on how it was collected and what human resources you have for this work.

4.1.4   Keynote Speakers
Did the keynote achieve what was expected? If not, what can be done for next time? Consider how keynotes are chosen and how they are prepped on the conference culture and audience.

4.1.5   Reception, Banquet and/or Other Special Events
Ask, for each, was it worthwhile? What did people take from these events? Look at responses on the evaluation form as well as the informal feedback. It is hoped that there will be some special moments at events such as these, some sort of 'sparkle' that 'makes the conference' for some or many people. If you do not see this, think about how to enhance these aspects next time.

4.1.6   The Culture of a Conference
Organizers and participants may have different views on some aspects of a conference that are hard to put into words. One of us when at a particular conference for the first time was unprepared for the style of questioning after a session. Taking on more of a 'heckling' quality, it seemed to be a form of 'one upmanship' in terms of tricky questions. On another occasion one of us, while on the executive of a society that ran an annual smaller conference, heard from some new participants that it felt 'cliquey'. This was hard to hear as we felt it was so very friendly. But it was worth considering and, where possible, asking people to explain more so that this annual event could be(come) what we, the society and the organizers saw it as and wished it to be.

5   Make an Impact Beyond the Conference

There are a number of ways to build on the momentum of the conference after it is over. It could involve the same people who registered for the main conference, or others. Chapter 9 speaks to related topics.

Pre- and post-conference activities are often built into conference planning. These may be mostly academic, such as workshops that are invited or part of the conference call. They could be visits to parts of campus, such as a new facility, lab, classroom or building.

Often a recreational excursion attracts participants to come early and/or stay after the main conference is over. This can be an otherwise missed chance to see the natural world and network informally with conference delegates. See Wright, Cassidy, and Monette (2013) and Cassidy, Wright, Strean, and Watson (2015) for descriptions of a long-running day-long paddling workshop that is associated with an annual conference.

A writing retreat can be organized by separate registration. See Volume 8, Issue 2 of *The Canadian Journal for the Scholarship of Teaching and Learning* http://www.cjsotl-rcacea.ca/ for publications resulting from work done by collaborative writing groups after the 2016 STLHE conference.

Some conferences invite papers to be submitted based on conference sessions. See http://tinyurl.com/yccahu86 for such peer-reviewed papers published annually since 2008. Other conferences publish proceedings of papers presented, often requiring one to also review one or more papers for consideration. These are excellent ways to build on the hard work presenters did to submit to a conference, prepare and present. Now they can share their work with a much wider audience.

In addition to what has been described above, what effect is there, perhaps on the wider community, as a result of this conference? It could be within the host institution(s) if internal, or broader if national or international. As the anecdote introducing this chapter suggests, consider inviting those who recently presented from your institution to reprise or adapt their session in a series organized by the teaching support centre, within your own department, or informally at a lunch event.

Chapter 4 describes positive impacts expressed by those attending conferences. Cassidy and Poole (2016) note some ways that respondents, building on a conference experience, brought added value to their institution. For example, ask a conference keynote or workshop leader to stay on a day or two more to present at your institution, and/or to live-stream to other institutions, further broadening the impact.

The possibilities are near-endless. Serving on a conference committee affords new networking opportunities, for research, teaching, publishing. Attending a conference as a participant can inspire you to organize such an event at home. The effort you make to organize a small- or large-scale educational event such as a conference can expand into many offshoots that help enhance teaching, learning and scholarship. Your colleagues and your institution will be grateful.

References

Cassidy, A., & Poole, G. (2016). Using social network analysis to measure the impact and value of work that takes us beyond institutional boundaries. *International Journal for Academic Development, 21*(4), 323–336.

Cassidy, A., Wright, A., Strean, W. B., & Watson, G. (2015). The interplay of space, place and identity: Transforming our learning experiences in an outdoor setting. *Collected Essays on Learning and Teaching, 8,* 27–34. Retrieved from https://celt.uwindsor.ca/ojs/leddy/index.php/CELT/article/view/4242

Cassidy, A. L. E. V., & Simmons, N. (2009, February). *Conference pedagogy: Change can be good.* Educational Developers Caucus Conference, Durham College, Oshawa.

Ivie, R., & Czujka, R. (2007, November). What's your survey telling you? *Physics Today,* pp. 78–79. Retrieved from www.physicstoday.org

Krosnick, J. A., & Presser, S. (2010). Question and questionnaire design. In J. D. Wright, P. V. Marsden (Eds.), *Handbook of survey research* (2nd ed.). Bingley: Emerald Group Publishing Ltd.

Wright, A., Cassidy, A., & Monette, M.-J. (2013). Paddling through time: Learning for life in the coastal zone. *Society for Teaching and Learning in Higher Education Newsletter, 2013*(62), 1–2. Retrieved from http://stlhesapes.wildapricot.org/Resources/Documents/Issue%2062.pdf